Books by Ralph Charell

*How I Turn Ordinary Complaints
into Thousands of Dollars
A Great New Way to Make Money
How to Get the Upper Hand
How to Make Things Go Your Way*

Ralph
Charell

The
Magic
of **Thinking**
Rich

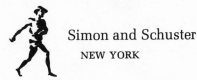

Simon and Schuster
NEW YORK

Published by Simon and Schuster
A Division of Gulf & Western Corporation
Simon & Schuster Building
Rockefeller Center
1230 Avenue of the Americas
New York, New York 10020

SIMON AND SCHUSTER and colophon are trademarks of
Simon & Schuster
Designed by Irving Perkins Associates
Manufactured in the United States of America
1 2 3 4 5 6 7 8 9 10

Library of Congress Cataloging in Publication Data

Charell, Ralph.
The magic of thinking rich.

1. Finance, Personal.   I. Title.
HG179.C535   332.024   80-26089

ISBN 0-671-42376-2

Contents

I

Bread and Chocolate

Some of the people with whom you are already acquainted have a net worth in excess of a million dollars, lawfully acquired without benefit of gift, inheritance or marriage. These people were your school chums or neighbors or colleagues or friends or professional consultants or fellow club members. They are no more intelligent than you. They are no more competent. They are no more deserving. Why are these people and thousands of other wealthy individuals who have amassed their own private fortunes, and their families, enjoying the best that money can buy, while you and your family are making do and doing without? Is there a magic to acquiring and keeping big money and, if so, how can you benefit from it?

There is a magic to putting together vast wealth and how to become an adept practitioner of this magic is the subject of this book. However, *The Magic of Thinking Rich* is not intended for every random reader who happens to pick it up. My objective in writing *The Magic of Thinking Rich* is to reach perhaps the one reader in ten who is initially attracted to its subject matter, those for whom the acquisition of great personal wealth is a passion, not a passing fancy.

If the book delivers on its promise to this specific group and these opening remarks discourage in advance most of those who would not find it useful, it will endure and be of great value to a relatively small but cumulative readership and its author will not only be rewarded amply, but will have spared himself some of the slings and arrows of the outraged non-fortuned, the sound of fury from those for whom the book was never intended. Good health is a desideratum to which all may aspire, but a good health club is not equally valuable to all of its prospective members. So it is also with money and The Magic of Thinking Rich.

If you think gout and gluttony are the accompanying signs of wealth, The Magic of Thinking Rich is not for you. If you're content to be comfortably well off, The Magic of Thinking Rich is not for you. The Magic of Thinking Rich is addressed to those who feel bereft without big money but great personal wealth has so far eluded them, or it met their outstretched fingertips fleetingly, only to dart off out of reach.

If you feel deprived without vast wealth, regardless of how well others may thing you're doing, if you can't eat a McDonald's hamburger or use a Bic pen or shave with a Gillette blade or carry ordinary luggage without a twinge of pain, if you never travel first class or first cabin but you know these are the only ways to go, if your table is ordinary, but you'd love to be served the best food and drink in a setting of your own fine crystal and silver and china, if you know there's something better out there and you yearn for it, then no matter how humble your station, The Magic of Thinking Rich is written for you. It is for those for whom not having great wealth means withdrawal symptoms even if they've never had big money in their lives.

Big money is many things to many people. It is a tool and a tranquilizer, it is warmth and safety, it is privacy and comfort, it is ease and luxury. It is freedom from want and fear. It is never having to say you're sorry to yourself or to those you love. It is entree and serenity. It is the best of the world's goods and services and a life of great opportunities and pleasures for you and your heirs forever.

Those who have learned they can produce a desired result through their own efforts do precisely that again and again. They are the people who make things go their way. They will improve whatever they touch and their lives will be active and productive and they will prosper.

Millions of others, however, lack this magic. There are myriad explanations for this life-dimming lack. In many cases, the reason is simply that the early models these people observed were not success models. They had a front-row, seven-days-a-week seat from which they could not only learn how to fail, they could not help but allow these lessons to become part of themselves. This is the real tragedy behind the needless despair of millions and it feeds on itself and is passed about like a communicable disease and handed down to unborn, unsuspecting victims. This is the attitudinal "ghetto" that so perniciously separates the "have-nots" from the "haves."

Yet there is a way to break out of this ghetto and come into your own, and some are finding it every day. You are a human being, not some inert material only capable of repeating the same bad programming over and over again, however unrewarding, wasteful and self-destructive. You have the ability to pull the plug on this programming that silently drains your spirit and remorselessly cuts you down. Indeed, if you and those closest to you are to be happy, healthy, long-lived and prosperous, you must do so, and the sooner the better for all concerned.

Lest the reader think he or she is being offered easy preachment or vague theory, let me present some of my personal credentials. I have personally tasted the thrill of victory and the agony of defeat. At different times of my life I've lived both as a prince and a pauper. I have traveled widely on lavish expense accounts and I've panhandled in the street in order not to go hungry. I've been wined and dined in private dining rooms by high financiers and bankers and I've received disconnect notices from the telephone company for nonpayment of bills. I've given away $175 fountain pens with 18-carat gold points and I've not had the price of a ball-point in my pocket. I've been driven from city to city in chauffeured limousines and I've hitchhiked home in a truck because I didn't have a nickel for the bus. I've been a guest at some of the finest hotels in the world, used their hot tubs and health clubs and sent back some of their most lavish room-service meals and I've slept in a mission on skid row and drunk black coffee that tasted like mud and eaten some "library paste" pie for breakfast. I've worn $200 shoes, $400-plus custom suits and Chinese silk shirts and I've also worn torn tennis shoes and tattered underwear and suits and coats whose poor fabrics were thin and shiny with wear. I've owned and operated a securities firm on Wall Street that bore my name and devised a method of trading with my own money that bagged and pocketed fifty-one consecutive profits within five months and I have been stretched so thin I had to meet a $245 margin call by liquidation. I've owned more than a metric ton of silver bullion and advised millionaires on their investments and I've had to borrow from a finance company. I've been gently tanned in vacation paradises and, hard-hatted, I've dug ditches in the desert under a blistering sun in a company-owned town.

I know what money is and how it is made and what it can buy and how it feels to have a great deal of it. I also know the look and the sting of empty checkbooks and the quiet despair of stacks of overdue bills and a family to support and their looming doubts and unvoiced fears.

In the following pages, you will see how to experience the exhilaration of success, while the sterile tundra of frustration and failure fade from memory. You will learn how

to ally your efforts with those who can multiply these efforts, to your mutual benefit, and how to avoid those who,
however well-intentioned, will only cancel your efforts
and keep you mired and out of the money. You will assign
a ratchet to your serious money so it doesn't seep into the
drainage. You will set out on a voyage toward your own
big piece of the pie. This time, however, you will take with
you a reliable map and compass and all the provisions you
will need and this time, too, you will leave behind all of
the ballast and detritus that have held you back and worn
you ragged in the past.

You will learn to let your mistakes make you not angry
but thoughtful, for one's own honest error can be a great
classroom, second only to apprenticeship to a master. You
will not let your errors deter or discourage you from playing the game for error committed once saves much time in
becoming effective and the more errors you commit only
once, the sooner you will reach your full height and depth.

Spirit and attitude are important. Big money is a serious
pursuit but you should not be overly serious in its quest
for it comes in greatest abundance to those who have a zest
and an enthusiasm for what they are about and it shuns
the dour.

Money, unlike water, seeks not its own level but a level
above its own. To facilitate the flow of funds in your direction, you will learn how to place yourself at a higher level
than their source. You will learn how to build your personal fortune to last forever without taking forever to do
so. In the quest for great wealth you will learn not to close
your mind to possibilities far afield and to be equally open
to opportunities before your eyes. At an absolute minimum, the entire world is your playing field. Money is such
an abundant by-product it can be the result of almost any
endeavor.

Big money has a rhythm of its own. Not everybody needs
its sound and feel and high step and kick, and those who

do have icebergs of private reasons why. If you've ached and hungered to join this minuet but you're still sitting at a side table or standing at the bar or pressing your nose up against the window glass outside, perhaps your turn is at hand.

II

Big Money: The Inner Game

Before you become rich, you must be *prepared* to become rich. This preparation is a rather simple, but absolutely necessary, process in the accumulation of a great personal fortune. Nobody would reasonably expect to wade into the English Channel and swim across it, without preparation. Even the most gifted natural athletes require preparation before their potential greatness is realized. The best magicians in the world need much preparation before they are able to walk out onto a stage and mystify and astound us. So, too, money magic requires preparation and the process may be even more subtle than that of other preparations, for money is often confused with other commodities and it has myriad individual, privately coded, meanings.

If you haven't paid much attention to the inner aspects involved in accumulating big money and you aren't one of fortune's favorites who learned them, almost genetically, beginning in the crib or by apprenticeship to a money-magnetic magnate, you will nevertheless be able to catch up if you quiet your mind and stop trying until you are adequately prepared to move forward. There are two elements in the inner game of amassing your own personal fortune. [First, you must be and remain completely convinced, and harbor no doubt whatsoever within you, that the acquisition of big money is a worthwhile endeavor] [Second, you must be and remain completely convinced, and harbor no doubt whatsoever within you, that you are worthy of the acquisition of big money. In short, you must completely assimilate the unwavering belief that big money is good enough for you and that you are good enough for big money. This is the indispensable, often overlooked, combination of magic ingredients which will make your money soufflé rise.

Some prepare for acquiring wealth through a gradual, osmotic process, by observing the success of others at close range over a long period of time. Others, not so privileged to witness such successes early and often, learn to disqualify themselves through a similar process.

Societal pressures also eliminate many from the ranks of the big-moneyed. Few people, for example, are fully aware they may have mixed feelings about becoming rich. They discount or ignore years of conditioning into their minds the association of big money with something undesirable or evil. We hear of "filthy lucre." We are told, however inaccurately, that "money is the root of all evil." We are shown stereotypical characterizations in the mass media (often skillfully cast and artfully made up and accoutered) of villainous mortgagees, flinthearted bankers, debauched millionaires, dishonest financiers, avaricious business people, robber barons, "fat cats" (portrayed by obese actors of virtually behemoth proportions), unscrupulous "wheeler-dealers" and victimizing landowners, and we read of similar characters and conjure them in our own minds. We learn of "blood money," sweatshops, profiteers, the selling of one's soul and other forms of self-prostitution. On the other hand, the depiction of scores of dignified laborers and other happy, healthy, hardworking, poor but honest folk and their families, sometimes with musical accompaniment, tends to make poverty an attractive alternative to wealth within our own minds.

Thus, for whatever reasons, and there are many motives, money is given a widely disseminated bad press and it becomes, in the minds of some, tainted, repugnant, a forbidden fruit. One of the effects of this kind of conditioning is to develop, at a level of the mind below conscious awareness, a strong aversion to the accumulation of a large personal fortune on the part of an individual so affected, while at the conscious level, he or she stoutly proclaims the wish to be rich.

The result of this simultaneous attraction toward, and repulsion from, the acquisition of wealth is a series of uncoordinated, halfhearted, short-lived, often convulsed, attempts at fortune-building, all of which efforts are soon neutralized. Making big money does not necessarily require you to expend a great effort over a long period of time. It does, however, require you to have and maintain a strong sense of purpose and to harbor no internal divisions, no subconscious tugs-of-war.

The antidote for such self-imposed limitations lies in bringing the submerged negative thoughts and feelings you may have about becoming rich to the surface, where you can expose these self-defeating elements to the scrutinizing beacon of reason. Discover the origin of these negative notions. Like many other perfectly good items that may be ill-used, money is not inherently bad or evil. Find harmonious agreement with the following two propositions: First, you will acquire your wealth fairly, honestly and creatively, without taking from anybody more than your share, nor giving less to anybody than his or her due, wholeheartedly giving full weight and measure and value and creating goods and services of real worth and purpose in the process. Second, you will use your wealth to good purpose, to help yourself and others, and never to harm or abuse anybody, yourself included.

It is well to think quietly of these two propositions at least twice daily for a month, setting aside a couple of minutes each time during which to sit or lie relaxed, in a comfortable position, with your eyes closed. Another excellent way of breaking the conditioning effects that have produced your subconscious antipathy to becoming rich is through self-hypnosis. This process offers a means of finding and eliminating the bad programming in your subconscious mind and substituting it with a deep-seated, positive attitude toward a wealthy you. There are many books on this subject in public libraries or they may be purchased at reasonably low cost. One presentation of how to use self-hypnosis is *Self-Hypnotism* by Leslie M. LeCron, available in a Signet paperback edition. Some friends and I have used self-hypnosis to good effect in breaking the smoking habit.

After you have cast out all of the negative thoughts and feelings you may have been harboring about whether money was good enough for you, it remains for you to guard against their return. In this connection, you must be careful not to overgeneralize. If and when you see an actual or fictional example of a person acquiring or using money improperly, be consciously aware this does not imply *all* people (or any other person) will or must follow suit, nor does it imply *this* person will or must continue to acquire or use money improperly. Moreover, it implies nothing whatever about *you.* You do not and will not acquire or use your wealth improperly and there is nothing inherently bad or evil about money.

If you are satisfied that you are, and will remain, completely convinced, and harbor no doubt whatsoever within you that the acquisition of big money is a worthwhile endeavor, you are ready to master the second element of your inner preparation for wealth: that you are, and will remain, completely convinced and harbor no doubt whatsoever within you that you are worthy of the acquisition of big money. In order to assimilate the unshakable belief that you are good enough for big money, it is necessary to examine and correct certain thought patterns you have created which have kept, and are still keeping, big money from reaching you, and which, by virtue of unchallenged repetition, have become part of your general attitude toward money and which you reflect on a regular basis.

You create linguistic thought patterns that are either expressed as speech or remain as communications to yourself in the form of unvoiced thoughts. These thousands and thousands of spoken and unspoken communications are of enormous importance in determining your life-style. They are characteristic of you. Their style is your style. What you say to yourself (and to others) is a major determinant of your life.

In a later chapter, the effects of what you say to others (and how you say it) will be examined closely. First, however, it is well to become aware of the profound effects your inner speech, your thoughts, have on your life, for not only are your communications with others influenced and shaped by your communications with yourself, but also the greatest and most long-lasting improvements come from the inside out. Your thoughts are integral to your self-image and to the way you manage yourself. In addition, once you put your own house in order, literally and figuratively, you are well on your way to a harmonious and mutually profitable relationship with the rest of the world.

This inner speech, your thoughts, can cause you to be rich or poor, loved or unloved, happy or unhappy, attractive or unattractive, powerful or weak, secure or insecure, joyful or joyless, healthy or unhealthy, spontaneous or rigid, creative or uncreative, productive or unproductive, fulfilled or unfilfilled, whole or fragmented, and so on. As all but the first dichotomy are beyond the scope of this book, the relevant comments that follow are specifically directed to the furtherance of your inner preparation for becoming rich.

Your inner voice is a powerful shaper of your life. It interprets the world for you and annotates and edits the events and circumstances you encounter in a way designed to maintain your view of the world and of yourself, undisturbed. It is so efficient a homeostatic factor in your life, you are often completely unaware of its presence but it is with you wherever you go, even when its attempts at aid and comfort, by keeping you in status quo, are to your most serious disadvantage. Once you are fully aware of the force and effect of these internal messages and how insidiously they operate to keep you away from getting and keeping big money, you will be ready to stop transmitting self-defeating internal messages and to substitute other messages that will facilitate the acquisition of your personal fortune. In effect, you will not merely be erasing these old, ill-conceived and self-limiting tapes, you will be recording over them new, well-designed, constructive messages that will further your purpose of acquiring your own personal fortune.

You must resolve, completely and irrevocably, to stop discriminating against yourself in thought (and speech) as it concerns the concept of you as a person of wealth and status. Henceforth, you should never think, or say, of any goods or services: "Thus and so is only for rich people" or "I can't afford that." You must take firm hold of the thought that no goods and services are too good for you. Goods and services are only goods and services. You are a unique, precious, irreplaceable and wonderful human being and the scale of your value is incomparably greater than the scale of value of any and all mere goods and services. You are already able, or can easily learn, to enjoy the best that money can buy and, given the possession of vast wealth, you might or might not, at your election, choose to buy this or that example of the world's goods and services. Remember, we are considering only the purchase of goods and services, not the creation of music or art, or some such. You must accept the fact that there is absolutely no reason why you shouldn't be able to open your mind to an appreciation of the best and the finest goods and services the world has to offer.

Many people approach programs designed to help them with skepticism. Other programs they began in the past may not have yielded the desired results no matter how hard they wished it otherwise. Perhaps the burden these other programs had to overcome was an internal division in the minds of those for whom the programs did not work and this was simply too great a burden to sustain. It would, similarly, be a mistake to attempt to amass your own personal fortune with less than a wholehearted commitment.

To minimize the number, and the tendency to exaggerate the effects, of setbacks, you must learn to close ranks with yourself. You must cast out all divisions within and admit none. These internal divisions often produce a continual crossfire, in which the fragmented self repeatedly ambushes itself. Launched from the perfect vantage point from which to inflict maximum damage, even small-scale internal ambushes may produce a wide assortment of self-imposed mental and physical penalties and punishments. These, in turn, weaken your will and neutralize and nullify your efforts to improve your position, "confirming" your unworthiness. Then the wheel and the rack turn anew.

All self-doubts, all divisions within, must be removed and estopped from reentry. If you are to become rich, your will and your purpose must be undivided. You must be 100 percent behind yourself. The moment you become less than 100 percent completely committed to your goal of wealth, and more than zero percent divided against yourself, your entire effort is poised to spiral into the ground. Any reversal, even a temporary setback that is part of the normal cycle, tends to become exaggerated. A single element of doubt and uncertainty, introduced into your own mind, where it can exert its greatest negative effect, can scuttle the best-laid plans.

Like the overcoming of the body's defenses against disease, the process is insidious. The normal, healthy human body harbors, and is surrounded by, a great number of disease germs at all times. Ordinarily, the body's immune systems and other natural defenses against disease are sufficient to maintain health. However, a lowering of bodily defenses, which can be caused by physical or psychological factors, or a combination thereof, can be enough to swing the balance against the maintenance of good health, and produce pathology and even death.

In the same way, given any shelter within, at times of stress, when your natural defenses are lowered by fatigue, illness, disappointment, reversal or setback, even the slightest divisive element within becomes active, multiplies, gains a toehold, a foothold, takes the high ground, neutralizes your resolve and stops your progress toward your personal fortune. As disease germs exert their most virulent effects from within your own body, divisive elements within your own mind are of the greatest potential harm.

This is the real danger involved in harboring any, even the slightest, doubt, uncertainty or division within, the reason your inner preparation for wealth must be complete, without a single chink, seamless, before you may proceed to become wealthy. In addition to thus protecting not only your flanks but your very center and, indeed, your entire position, by casting out all divisive elements and keeping them out, you are able to move forward unimpeded, strongly, wholeheartedly, concentrated, focused, on point, without wavering, waddling or vacillating, to maximum effect, toward your own big piece of the money pie. No longer will you experience this or that minor upset as an earthquake. No longer will you have to seek outside confirmation for your every move or decision.

In significant ways, you are still, almost certainly, acting out a role in a drama, many key parts of which were not scripted by you. A number of your basic attitudes and beliefs about yourself and the world have been internalized during your years of infancy and childhood. Regardless of how well they may have served you in the past, some of these attitudes and beliefs are no longer serviceable. This is true regardless of the motives or intentions of any of those who handed down these attitudes and beliefs to you, or even of whether they were handed down to you intentionally or not, or whether you received them as transmitted and are now properly decoding, storing and retrieving the messages that make up these attitudes and beliefs. In this way, you are allowing your past to determine your future and keep you from big money. This is an unnecessary consequence.

The human mind ordinarily stores all of the old tapes and provides access to them. When you are stressed, it is all too easy to order up some of the old, unserviceable tapes of doubt, disappointment and surrender and to play them into your conscious mind. This, despite the fact that these messages, tested in the light of reason and experience, not only failed to provide what it is you sought, but they helped unstick your own resolves and actually facilitated the very disappointments that prompted their call from storage.

The pattern is fairly clear. The particular upset was real and immediate. Ultimate success was viewed as illusory or at a point so far in the future the time path that led to it was cluttered and obscured. Routine setbacks were received as evidence of personal unworthiness. There was a self-defeating tendency to identify the self with the setback, to draw unwarranted conclusions and to make overgeneralizing pronouncements. For example, when overreacting to an error you may have made, you might have said of yourself: "What an idiot!" instead of saying or thinking a compassionate, understanding formulation more in accord with the facts, such as; "I am a worthy person who erred."

You have the ability to change all, or any parts, of these old tapes, but first you need to become aware of which messages are no longer serving your purposes. When you are relaxed, you can become aware of some of these unworkable beliefs more easily, and of how they operate to keep you from realizing your goal of big money. One clue to these messages is to examine yourself closely when you get upset and discover what message or messages you are calling up from storage during, and immediately prior to, the upset. Another clue will be provided by your body if you can discover what circumstances, including your inner communication with yourself, occur immediately prior to your becoming ill, or taken with any internal disorder, bodily ache, pain or stiffness. Careful examination and note-taking should yield a valuable pattern. With awareness, of course, the next step is to defuse or *disconnect* the source of the upset from the result of it, that is, the harmful effects on you.

For example, suppose you have been carrying about with you some unserviceable notions about money and you discover that a large stack of unpaid bills is usually followed by your becoming ill or shrill. Suppose, too, that the message you are telling yourself is something like this: "Worthy people pay their bills on time. I cannot afford to pay my bills on time. Therefore, I am not a worthy person." As an unworthy person, in your own mind, you are, of course, more likely to create additional problems for yourself, such as illness, accidents, bad personal relationships, etcetera.

These damaging messages tend to become deeply ingrained by virtue of their repetition to yourself and others. They are thus placed in a readily accessible part of your mental filing system. There are two good techniques for eliminating the tolls of these messages. The first involves an understanding that there is no outside causal link between an upsetting circumstance and its damaging effects upon you. This means that in the above example the mere fact that you are unable to pay your bills at this time does not mean that you must become ill or suffer any of the other consequences. A stack of unpaid bills is nothing more than that and any overgeneralizing statements about yourself that this occasions are unwarranted and needlessly damaging. Thus, in this example, you may take the position that there is a stack of unpaid bills, they will, presumably, be paid in due course, and I don't have to become ill.

Another way of eliminating the harmful effects of these messages is to record another message over them. Thus, instead of retelling tales of woe and upset to yourself and others, grinding the unpleasantness ever deeper into your own psyche, first you stop repeating the stories to others. This will help your standing with others because the repetition of tales of woe presents you as a person to whom woeful events happen and this is perceived by others as a shortcoming in you. Then, instead of repeating these tales to yourself and thinking of, and dwelling on, their unpleasant ramifications, think of the circumstances that led to the upset and then imagine, not the actual event as you remember it, but the happiest ending possible in your fantasy. Everybody loved you. They rolled out the red carpet. You received ten times more than you expected and fifty times more than anybody else ever received, and so on. This, of course, will not change the past event but it will break its damaging hold on you by getting a lot of unproductive static out of your mind and eliminating the tendency to keep repeating the same error.

This will serve to harmonize and solidify your character, and it is your character that creates your destiny. Your character is the tool with which you approach the world. If it is defective or brittle or unbalanced or dull or entrusted with barnacles, it will be incapable of producing its best results for you. It will constrict and dim your life. Your zest for living will evaporate. You will feel pain and loss and anxiety and this will lead to additional chinks and imperfections in your character. These, in turn, will be reflected in your attitudes and actions and the process will feed on itself, as your life winds down to a joyless existence.

On the other hand, an inner preparation for acquiring wealth will leave you strengthened and purified. Instead of repeating a surprisingly small number of characteristic errors that have kept you from amassing your personal fortune, you are now ready to proceed from strength.

Summary

work on self limiting belief
use uplifting affirmations
Know that you are worthy...
you trust money and money
trusts you. d use money
as a tool for the good of all.
Put 100% into you. you must
be secure in who you are.
No internal dialoge that plagues
you with its negativity.

My programing comes from my family
and their narcissists who projected
their reality onto me. d am free!!

III

The Big Money Pull of High-Density People

If you are entirely satisfied that your inner preparation is complete, you are ready to look at the part of the magic of thinking rich I call "money consciousness" and "high density." I say "look at" because an important aspect of your acquiring both a money consciousness and high density of your own involves your powers of observation. A money consciousness, an indispensable component of high density, is a fully awake, sensory awareness and appreciation of what money is, what it can do for you, how it is made in large amounts, and by whom.

An understanding of the elements that comprise high density is extremely valuable for several reasons. People whose money consciousness is not evolved repeatedly underestimate the impact of their presentation of themselves as a function of their lack of money success. They are often not even aware they are being observed by others. Their ostrichlike lack of perception does not, of course, ensure their remaining unobserved. It would be useful to have on hand a virtual checklist of characteristics possessed by high-density people. Once you become aware that you are presenting yourself in certain ways that drastically limit your opportunities for wealth, you may begin where you find yourself and adjust your presentation of yourself accordingly. As you eliminate low-density behavior from your repertoire, and begin to think and act as a high-density person, your breadth as a money magician will automatically expand. You will be making it easier for riches to seek and find you, and for those with money to repose greater confidence in you, and to listen to you with greater interest as it concerns money. Thus, your acquisition of a money consciousness and high density will act as a facilitator and conduit for your becoming rich.

In addition, you will be able to distinguish quite easily those people who have a money consciousness and high density from those who do not. This is important, for the efforts of the former ripen and mature, as if by magic, into great financial success, whereas those who do not possess these attributes find it exceedingly difficult to acquire and keep a lot of money. After your own money consciousness and high density have been developed, you will be able to seek out, and enter into wealth-producing relationships with, those who will expedite your becoming wealthy and to avoid involvements in profit-oriented ventures with those who will short-circuit your plans and impede your progress.

You may have seen a number of people struggle for years, in vain, to amass wealth. Or, you may be familiar with accounts of impecunious persons who became "instant millionaires" via lottery winnings but who were ill at ease with money. Their wealth became a source of discomfiture. Before long, they resumed their humble jobs and once again were accepted by their former neighbors and co-workers. They felt better in modest surroundings than they ever did in the midst of plenty. These people, both those whose efforts remain uncrowned by success and those who feel out of place with money, lack a money consciousness, an important component of high density, without which there can be no legerdemain, no money magic.

This quality we are calling money consciousness is not only a catalytic agent in fortune-building, it also acts to enhance the enjoyment of wealth. However, a money consciousness does not become truly yours through the memorizing of certain formulations or the rote learning of certain facts or even by the putting of certain principles into practice. Your money consciousness is evolved through a curious process of assimilation, in much the same way your native language becomes a part of you. Sensory data and other material "outside" the self are processed into elements such as understanding, attitude, spirit, and so on, which you carry about "inside" of yourself and which become integral parts of yourself, like the body-building elements in good, wholesome food. The words "outside" and "inside" are in quotation marks because from certain points of view the distinction we commonly make between "outer" and "inner" is not recognized, but further consideration of this concept goes beyond the scope of this work.

In the true money magician, this process of assimilating a money consciousness precedes the creation of wealth. It is not the turning of this or that phrase, or even complete fluency in your native language, that makes it a part of you. It is the fact that you think in it, dream in it, it expresses you, it is a living part of you—that makes it your own. In the same way, the magic in the magic of thinking rich is not in the trick of acquiring this or that packet of money. The magic is in the magician.

As set forth near the beginning of this chapter, the first step in acquiring a money consciousness involves your powers of observation. How unerringly, for example, would you be able to select those who had amassed a personal fortune of their own from those who had not, in a steam room, on a public or private beach, in a hotel lobby, or anywhere else excessive environmental clues were not available? Can you distinguish from among a group who have not amassed great wealth those who possess the most potential as money magicians?

The ability to make these judgments accurately is important for a number of reasons, and it is worth developing. Accomplished money magicians and those with most potential to join their ranks, as already indicated, are your best allies in money-making ventures. Additionally, as you begin to focus your attention on the common denominators among those who are able to amass wealth, these similarities will serve as living textbooks, as it were, to guide you by example and to shorten the period of your own apprenticeship and internship.

A money consciousness, although indispensable, is but one element of the congeries of characteristics we are here calling high density. This special combination, or cluster, exerts a remarkable attraction for money in much the same way gravitation exerts an attraction on matter. All bodies in the universe, from the heavenly bodies down to the smallest particles of matter, have a mutual attraction for one another. This mutual attraction, or pull, toward one another, is in direct proportion to the masses of the bodies and varies inversely as the squares of the distances between them. The above is culled almost verbatim from *The Columbia Encyclopedia* in its entry on "gravitation" and it can be found in hundreds of other sources on the subject of Newton's law of gravitation. In this context, the term "mass" refers to the total quantity of matter in a body and "density" to the weight or mass of a unit volume of a substance. Thus, for example, if one matched pair of dice weighs more than another matched pair of equal volume, the heavier pair is also of greater density, of greater mass, and has a greater gravitational force, than the lighter pair. In short, the pair of higher density has a greater attraction or "pulling power" on all the bodies in the universe than the pair of lower density.

There is, I contend, a cluster of common characteristics packed into people who are able to create wealth that gives them a "higher density," as it were, and hence a strong natural pull between themselves and big money. High-density people have a well-developed money consciousness to attract, select and focus on money-creating opportunities in the environment and to combine them into a package of energy, action, direction, talent, capital and other elements designed to produce profitable results.

The selection process is critical and high-density people rigorously screen out the unlikely projects of limited potential and those in which their contributions and functions are not clearly evident. They are aware that to fail to eliminate scrupulously these kinds of projects from serious consideration needlessly drains energy into projects of little or no return. It creates waste, wheel-spinning, futility, vacillation; it dampens the spirit and puts a strain on other aspects of living. Doubtful projects of this nature are reminiscent of the too oft-repeated needlessly cruel experiments in which a laboratory animal is rewarded with food for selecting one shape, say a square, and given an electric shock for selecting a recognizably different shape, say a circle. After the animal learns to distinguish the shapes and is conditioned to expect the square shape to yield food, the two shapes are gradually changed in the direction of congruence. The square becomes a succession of increasingly many-sided equilateral polygons; the circle becomes a succession of decreasingly many-sided equilateral polygons, until they are indistinguishable. By this time, the laboratory animal is confused and disoriented. It is reduced to vacillation, indecision, immobility, accompanied by great stress. Sometimes, the animal begins to act irrationally and self-destructively. It may even die.

This pattern of behavior, vacillation, indecision, immobility, accompanied by great stress, irrational and self-destructive behavior, is, unfortunately, not atypical of low-density people. High-density people, on the other hand, don't scatter and waste their resources. A favorable risk/reward ratio, that is, the potential reward or possible gain, in relation to the downside potential, or maximum possible loss, a formula sufficient to many, is a necessary, but by no means sufficient, condition for high-density people.

For example, if somebody offered a large payoff for successfully hurling a half-dollar across a wide river, given sufficient publicity, presumably there would be a large contingent of challengers. High-density people would not be much in evidence among their number. Notably absent, the latter would go right on doing what they do best. They are extraordinarily selective. They neither seek nor want free rides. Nor do they wish to waste their time or energy in pursuits not within the compass of their abilities to produce a result.

This is not to say that high-density people are not open to new ventures. They are, but they are not easily turned to projects that find no resonances within themselves. They prefer to be rewarded for the special contribution they can make to a project. They also like to exercise much control over the flow of events and communications of projects in which they engage and are disinclined to enter into activities in which these controls are held by others. They tend to cultivate intensely what they are best able to accomplish and most enjoy. They are not jacks-of-all-trades and do not clutch at doubtful opportunities far afield.

High-density people are extremely steadfast and resilient. Like pop-up toys, they rebound into position from upsets with hardly a hair out of place, and continue on their path. Nor are they easily flustered, and this combination gives them a rocklike steadiness and a solidity others with money notice and find attractive. They also tend to be active, energetic, persevering, hardworking. They are not continually nagged by self-doubt, nor do they indulge in second-guessing themselves. They are at ease with themselves and others. They are not disruptive or self-indulgent. They are extremely self-confident and, while they eschew braggadocio, they are convinced their efforts will be successful.

They are self-reliant and independent and enjoy seeing the results of their own efforts. They accept moderate risks, avoiding both foolhardy risks and the immobility of waiting about endlessly for sure things. Many who have inherited a modest fortune may be found in the latter category. Unable to live comfortably off the income their inheritance produces, with safety of principal assured, especially with inflation at recent rates, and unsure of their ability to add to their legacy through their own efforts, as they have never created or participated in their own successful projects and lack a sufficiently broad and deep base of experience, their legacy becomes a source of great personal insecurity. As a result, they live unnecessarily frugally, even as their inheritance is slowly whittled away.

Although high-density people can make money at almost any activity that attracts them, once they find a particular field of interest, they tend to concentrate their energies in it over a long period of time, developing their skills, broadening their knowledge and experience bases, establishing long-term, personal relationships with other leaders in the field, and creating a reputation for ability and character that attracts money to them whenever outside financing is deemed appropriate for expansion. They usually grow and develop from a scale of operations well within their capabilities to handle so that initial mistakes, if any, are small. A conservative beginning also keeps their need for outside capital relatively modest, even after allowing ample margins for safety. A small initial scale of operations also keeps the pressures of entering the field, whether by start-up or takeover, low.

As set forth above, they don't mind taking moderate or

prudent risks, but they are not high-rolling gamblers. They see no need to take excessively high risks, for they are confident they will succeed through their own efforts without unnecessary hazard. They are unwilling, in effect, to gamble on what they regard as a sure thing; namely, their own prospects in a field they know and like and in which they are willing to devote their time and energies.

High-density people are characteristically strong-willed and independent. They have the courage of their convictions, will stand behind their ideas and take the consequences. If convinced they are right, they are fully capable of "going it alone." They are decisive; they like to make decisions and take responsibility for them. Although they don't seek or need outside confirmations for their decisions, they like to see the concrete results of their efforts. As they don't need outside support for their decisions, they tend not to explain in detail, or even disclose, many of their decisions and the process by which they arrived at them. Over-explainers often thus reveal themselves as low-density people. Observant others will not fail to notice this telltale and opportunities for big money will not flow toward them.

In addition, although they are friendly, high-density individuals are not given to detailed explanations about their money-making activities, or of volunteering much autobiographical data. Whether consciously or not, they seem to appreciate that revealing the secret or precise method by which a seemingly magical result was created, somehow dispels the magic and diminishes the magician. They therefore keep the tapestry face-front so that precisely how and where each stitch was put into the pattern remains undisclosed. Thus, they sometimes appear as real-life Rumpelstiltskins, seemingly able to spin flax into gold, a most remarkable and magnetic ability.

Unlike many others, high-density people do not continually "sell" themselves. They do not bandy about accounts of their current activities. They don't like to make predictions about the future and their rare projections are usually understated. They involve themselves in the doing, not in the talking about the doing. Theirs is an active approach to the living of their lives, not alone in the aquisition of money. Although they are aware of, and concerned with, the wider ramifications of what they are about, they move in straight lines without endless philosophizing and soliloquizing.

High-density people conduct themselves as fully operational, self-contained units. If they were toys, they would be completely assembled, batteries included and installed. They seem to require nothing they cannot supply. They are self-sufficient and extremely resourceful. They follow their instincts, which they have learned to trust, without fear. Their approaches to the solutions of problems are sometimes unconventional, innovative and inventive, but they are well founded on the solid bedrock of knowledge and experience, never on mere hope.

They have defined objectives. Although these objectives may sometimes change, high-density people know what they want and can measure where they are in relation to where they should be in order to achieve a particular objective. They monitor and track results as they become available and adjust their actions to the data with almost zero time delay. As they check results on a continuing basis, they are rarely surprised, and never overwhelmed by, events.

They are extraordinarily practical. If the results are not as planned, they adjust. They do not expect the world to adjust to their thinking. Their egos are not on the line. They don't have to prove that the world is off base and they had been right all along but some fluke caused the bad result. If the result is not up to expectations, they look to their own input and rethink it. They also don't attempt to fasten blame on others for bad results, nor do they try to justify their original plan by rationalizing the less than expected performance, nor do they spend any time at all in what might have, should have, or would have, been, but for some entirely unforeseen events.

High-density people are great improvers of situations, take pride in going beyond past performance and routinely do so. They expect increasingly better results and greater profitability and they proceed from strength to strength, from success to success, most of the time. They also know how to close deals and, without unseemly or undue haste, they are usually able to make steady progress toward a closing. They are tortoises with enough of the hare bred in to be unbeatable at any distance.

Although their standards are high, the goals they set for themselves are moderate. When these goals are reached or surpassed, they set moderately higher goals, like the resetting of the bar by a high jumper or pole-vaulter after a successful effort. They tend to produce skeins of successes in measured steps rather than discrete leaps. The process is something like lifting a baby steer daily until its maturity, instead of trying to lift the grown animal without the benefit of the intervening daily, gradually increasing, lifts.

They are also honest. They have confidence in their own abilities and skills to produce the results they have planned and they have pride in their reputation and integrity. They have no need to cheat. They are purposeful, not aimless, but they are also composed and unhurried. They don't run to answer telephones, they don't keep looking at their watches. They are self-contained, self-controlled, and they don't present themselves or their plans or ideas until they are ready to do so. They set their own tempo.

High-density people are comfortable with money and, significantly, they do not allow themselves to be thrown off stride if their supply of it becomes short, as rarely happens. They regard such events as temporary cash-flow imbalances that their efforts will put right before long. They do not take it personally. It is simply a fact like any other, not a statement about their worthiness nor an indictment of any kind. Their equanimity remains intact. They go on about their business unruffled.

As money is a familiar tool to them, they understand prices and values and the distinctions between these concepts. Although they can well afford the highest-priced, top-of-the-line item and often buy it, there are times when they may consider it so overpriced in relation to another item easily substituted for it, they may decide to buy the latter. They do not lock themselves into a rigid commitment or need for a specific item at any price and they don't mind comparison shopping if it is warranted. As they respect (but do not revere) money, they are not profligate with it.

High-density people attract others in much the same way heavenly bodies of great density attract satellites: they are generally pulled, not to their bosom, but into an orbit about them. Information flows freely toward high-density people, sometimes coupled with advice. These data are sifted and sorted out, then discarded, modified, used or stored. They are not simply taken at face value but are subjected to a process similar to that used by a combination of line and staff generals in order to arrive at an optimal tactical plan and to modify overall strategy, if necessary. While the data come in from many sources, the decision remains in the hands of high-density people.

As you read and reread and consider the specific qualities of high-density people, picture in your mind the people you know who have amassed their own personal fortunes. Decide which of these qualities they possess and notice the absence of their opposites. All of these high-density attributes are observable and, consciously or unconsciously, other people with money notice whether we appear to be high- or low-density. Moneyed people feel more comfortable with high-density people and they will join forces with you and help you in money-making ways if you comport yourself as a high-density person.

As high-density people attract money and money-making opportunities that are real and big, and repel spurious and wasteful "opportunities," low-density people exhibit the opposite effect. If there is a wide gulf between your own deportment and that of high-density people, don't become discouraged. A long step in the right direction is to follow Hippocrates' precept: "First, do no harm." Stop repelling money and money-making opportunities by presenting yourself as a low-density person. When you have thus stanched the needlessly self-inflicted outflow and are healed and whole, you will then be ready to set about attracting riches with your own high-density properties.

IV

The Magic of Multiplying Money

The next step in your becoming an adept money magician is to grasp and assimilate the magic of multiplying money. Money is amenable to all of the basic arithmetic processes. Any sum of money can be added to, subtracted from, divided or multiplied. This is true not only of all amounts of money but also of all forms in which money may be kept and regardless of how derived, whether it results from work, investment, pension, allowance, allotment, or whatever may be the particular ways it comes to you.

The way to multiply your money is to choose the best "vehicles" for making you wealthy and to ally your (earned and unearned) moneymaking efforts with the people who can help you multiply your money, at the same time completely avoiding money involvements with all others. The magic in this approach lies in your ability to determine in advance the best "vehicles," and who can help you multiply your money and who cannot. This magic will serve you extraordinarily well. It will enable you to review past money successes and failures with new insight and to chart a clear course to an abundance of your own money. First, however, a few introductory remarks are in order.

How much you are financially rewarded is a close measure of the money value the system places on what you produce at any given time and place. This is so whether your income is earned or unearned and despite the opinion that the money value of what you or somebody else produces *ought* to be worth much more than that which another receives for what he or she produces. Whether or not a particular rock group, for example, *ought* to be paid more for a night's work than a college professor is paid in ten years is an important question but it is beyond the scope of this work. So, too, are considerations of psychic returns and values other than monetary that flow from this or that occupation outside the purview of this work.

Although how much money you receive is a close measure of the value the system places on what you produce, it may not be a precise measure. A given occupation may, for a time, because of certain temporary imbalances, be over- or underpriced. However, in a fluid and dynamic economy, these imbalances will tend to correct themselves by creating an additional supply of "overpriced" talent and a shortage of "underpriced" talent. Whether or not you accept the basic premise that, rightly or wrongly, the amount of money you are paid for what you do is a close measure of the money value the system places on the goods and/or services you directly or indirectly produce, the question remains as to how to increase the amount you get.

Whether you seek to produce more, produce it faster, improve its quality, or decide to enter a more lucrative field, there are strict limits to your own productivity, working alone. The best approach to multiplying your money, as stated earlier, involves combining your efforts with those of others who can help you, and avoiding money involvements with all others. You are already combining with others in efforts directed at multiplying money, whether or not you are fully aware of it. What is lacking in most cases, and what the material in this chapter will supply, is a way for you to increase your earned and unearned income by channeling your energies efficiently into the most profitable projects with the people who can help you, while, at the same time, steering you away from waste and loss associated with doubtful ventures and those who propose them.

Producing income is a cooperative process. If you are an employee, for example, your efforts are part of those of the business organization for which you work. If you operate an individual proprietorship, you may have a secretary or salespeople or others working for you. You probably have an accountant, an attorney, and others who advise you about money. If you are a principal in a partnership or own part of a corporation, you are obviously involved with others for the purpose of multiplying money. If you are an investor of any kind, you are probably dealing with brokers, advisers, or the like. If you are unemployed or wish to get a better job, you may use this magic to help you make money-multiplying alliances. Precisely which company, which department of that company, which partners or other principals, which attorney, broker, accountant, etcetera, your money-making efforts are combined with has an important effect on your long- and short-term financial return.

To take a simple example of money multiplication, say a doctor's time is producing a return of $100 per hour. He or she may decide to hire a receptionist/secretary and a technician at a rate of $10 and $15 per hour respectively, so that the doctor need not spend the more valuable, $100-per-hour time acting as a receptionist/secretary and technician, assuming the doctor could adequately acquit these assignments and ignoring the psychological effect on patients of having the doctor change roles in these ways and the greater efficiency of each through specialization.

Similarly, a lawyer might hire a junior lawyer at a much lower rate of remuneration than that of the senior lawyer so that the latter might spend the more valuable time on greater income-producing matters. In addition, the senior lawyer might bill the junior's time at $70 per hour and be paying perhaps $20 per hour. In effect, the senior buys the junior's time at wholesale rates and sells it to clients at retail. Although the economics are sound, not all receptionist/secretaries, technicians, and junior lawyers are equally good at multiplying their respective employer's incomes. Some, in fact, cause losses.

An art director, a copywriter and an account executive, each of whom is earning a good income as an employee of one or more advertising agencies, may decide to found their own advertising agency. If successful, their joint efforts may produce a company with gross billings in excess of a hundred million dollars annually. Actors, singers, musicians and other talented people have joined forces as teams or groups and dramatically increased their wealth. Sometimes, simply combining with a different agent or manager has produced a magical resurgence in a becalmed career.

The multi-billion-dollar advertising industry is built, in large part, on the idea that the producers of hundreds of billions of dollars worth of goods and services are less proficient at advertising them, and can increase their profits by allying with specialists who have little or nothing to do with the physical creation of the goods and services. On a smaller scale, an entrepreneur and a marketing expert may develop a good product or invention, dormant or moribund in the hands of its creator, into a highly profitable enterprise.

Individuals may also team up within an organization. Two or more people with similar or complementary abilities may, in concert, produce a much more valuable result than the sum of their individual efforts and such teams have catapulted their members into important corporate posts, with commensurately increased returns.

Money-oriented projects take on the personalities of their principal participants. This is why the principles involved in selecting the most likely alliances for the purpose of multiplying your money and avoiding all of the rest apply across the board to all money-oriented activities.

Obviously, not all opportunities for profit are equal and the merits of the specific opportunity are important and will be addressed later in this chapter. However, given only average ability to select the most likely opportunities, it is most important to be able to distinguish the people who can help you become wealthy from those who cannot. Even the best horses can be run out of the money by the wrong jockeys.

These principles also apply to employees, for how well the company does, and how well you will do as an employee of the company, is a function of the ability of its management to multiply money. This management ability is a necessary, but not a sufficient condition, for your department head within the corporation, like the wrong jockey, can produce a poor result for you if he or she is not a skilled money multiplier. For example, the department head of a large corporation with which I am familiar thought one of the primary functions of his job was to keep his department's budget relatively low and to stay within it; that is, never to exceed it regardless of circumstances. The company flourished and many of its executives prospered but he and his department were always underpaid and morale was low.

The magic of multiplying money will facilitate your making excellent progress within a corporation. You will not only be able to identify the best people with whom to ally your efforts, but you will also be able to present your-

self in ways that make you a worthy candidate for such
favorable alliances. In addition, you will be able to deal
with stockbrokers, real-estate brokers, lawyers, financial
advisers, tipsters and others in a way that magically hones
in on the best means by which you may multiply money
and avoid all of the alternates. You will also be able to
invest directly in profit-oriented ventures with a new confidence, whether your investment is limited to money only
or includes your time as well.

The fact that your money-producing efforts may be enhanced by favorable alliances is a well-established reality
of economic life. Equally true, but perhaps less apparent,
is the fact that your money-producing efforts may be ham-
pered, nullified, even turned to financial loss, by injudi-
cious alliances. The money subtracters and dividers are
apt to lead you into financial involvements in which you
lose money, waste time, run up expenses, divert your energies from profitable ventures, lower your resistance physically, and become emotionally upset.

These results are so predictable yet so easily avoided.
Several people tugging on the same end of the rope with
you obviously multiply your individual effort. Put them at
the opposite end of the rope and the result is quite different. Let them clutch at various points along the length of
the rope and tug in sundry directions and your best efforts
become only one of the forces to be factored into vectors
you never envisioned. The only chance you have to make
a small fortune with such money subtracters and dividers
is to begin with a large one.

Money multiplication involves large returns. In investments that require your money and little of your time, the
recommended objective is twenty times your money investment in a period of five to ten years. This focuses
the emphasis where it belongs; that is, on careful initial
selection, high return and patience. Despite oft-quoted, so-
called axioms, no doubt promulgated by brokers and others who have an interest in your buying and selling (as

distinguished from your holding your best investments, on which they ordinarily do not receive fees or commissions), to the effect that "nobody goes broke taking a profit," big money is not made by trading in and out of investments prematurely or by trying to scalp speculative situations for small profits.

For about nine years, I was a member of the so-called financial community and have observed thousands of people actively seeking profits by investing their money. Those who try to outguess or trade the market, by taking a series of relatively small profits, almost invariably lose money. The biggest money multipliers are those who make the right investment choices and exercise patience. Brokers, purveyors of get-rich-quick schemes and other tipsters may disagree all they care to with this advice but their interests and those of their clients are often in complete conflict, for their income is based directly or indirectly on the volume of transactions their clients generate yet the more their clients trade, the less likely they are to prosper.

If your objective is simply to derive income from investments with great safety of principal, the advice would be different. However, if your goal is to multiply money, the best way I know to do this via investment is to buy right and hold for the returns indicated above. In short-term gain situations (less than a year), the objective is gross profit (not including commissions and taxes) of two to two-and-a-half times your investment. In a 50 percent marginable security transaction, for example (the current availability), this gross profit would require a 50 to 75 percent price appreciation. You should, of course, remain current on your investment and be willing to sell it if it changes character to the point it no longer has the potential of a twentyfold increase or its lesser, short-term objective. Otherwise, continue to hold it. This approach places emphasis and attention on three elements: money multiplication, careful selection and patience.

It should be obvious that you don't have to multiply

your money by twenty too many times to become rich. Lest this objective appear to be too tall an order, particularly when compared with the much more moderate goals prescribed by conventional wisdom, let me cite some brief illustrations from my own experience. The first involves a stock that attracted me when it was selling at four dollars per share. It held advanced medical patents that seemed to me at the time to be years ahead of the field. I studied the company and decided this stock would almost certainly go to a price of forty, and probably to one hundred dollars per share. I bought some shares and took what many would regard as a decent profit (but nothing like the money multiplication discussed above). The stock, National Patent Development Company, advanced to a price of about two hundred dollars per share in approximately two years.

A second example involved a purchase of 34,992 troy ounces of silver bullion I made in October and December, 1971, at an average price of $1.402 per ounce. This was an approximately $50,000 position, which I took on 25 percent margin, at a cost of $12,500, and which I kept stored in a Swiss bank. Again, I took an excellent profit by almost any standards. Early in 1980, a little more than eight years later, that position had a market value as high as $1,750,000, one hundred forty times my investment.

Another example involves an investment I made in a privately owned company founded and operated by a friend of mine. Again, the situation appeared to have big potential for money multiplication. The company is prospering and my investment currently shows about a 300 percent appreciation. This time, however, I intend to follow the suggestion outlined above. I expect this holding to be worth not less than twenty times my original investment in the foreseeable future.

A final example involves an investment I made in a speculative equity that appeared to have excellent chances for extraordinary gains. The company was and is controlled and operated by a highly respected mining man who had been one of three men to parley eighty-three mining claims into some stock in perhaps the largest uranium mine in the world. That stock has a current value of approximately 37½ million dollars. This man has a reputation for integrity and a proven record of success in finding the rich mines he goes after. The company is on the move. I am sitting with a good profit and expect this holding to bring the kind of return indicated above.

In order to multiply your money most efficiently, all your money involvements should include money multipliers and exclude all others. As you set about substituting money multipliers for others in all of your business alliances in a prudent, unhurried fashion, you will be improving your current financial position and assuring your financial future. This applies to the management of your own company, the person to whom you report, your subordinates, co-workers, team members, financial advisers, brokers, partners, co-venturers, etcetera. If you are employed by a large company you don't control, it may be difficult to make all of these changes but you should never voluntarily enter into money alliances with non-money multipliers. A review of the previous chapter will serve you well in making this determination. Low-density people, with all due respect to their good qualities and to their humanity, almost invariably involve you in money-losing or stagnant situations. As a prudent first step, follow Hippocrates' advice (but apply it, not to your patients, but to yourself): "First, do no harm." This requires that you rigorously adhere to the decision never to enter into a money alliance with a low-density person. Make it your practice not to so much as discuss your money plans with them. If they initiate such discussions, be polite but don't prolong the conversation. Above all, never become financially involved with them.

Money multiplication on any serious scale will result from alliances with compatible, high-density people in projects that offer the kinds of rewards outlined elsewhere in this chapter. If you are diligent and patient with these projects you will multiply your money into substantial wealth. A couple of these alliances will make you rich and keep you on point, open to additional opportunities for wealth.

Compatibility is an important concept and its application to money multiplication should be considered carefully. Whether the other person complements your efforts by providing elements or strengths you lack, or simply augments your efforts through duplication of your strengths, the combination will function smoothly, synchronously and most profitably if there is an absence of friction and cross-purposes. As high-density can be estimated and identified in advance by observation, so, too, can compatibility.

Each of us perceives a small percentage of reality. This percentage is, perhaps, ten percent of what is actually there to be perceived. Of tremendous significance is the fact that each of us perceives a different ten percent! The greater the overlap of perception, the greater the chances for compatibility, other things being equal. This is not to say that relationships between and among people whose perceptions are markedly different are impossible. It is, however, my view that such relationships are more difficult to maintain and that if these difficulties are not recognized and actively minimized, the results these people produce, and certainly those that involve the multiplication of money, will be markedly limited.

It should be obvious that a symphony orchestra plays so well together because all of the players are musicians. Even a single non-musician sitting in a large orchestra will produce discord and chaos. So it is, too, with incompatible elements and the multiplication of money. A single incompatible person will almost invariably diminish and divert your best efforts.

There are myraid individual differences between and among people. These differences should be understood and respected. Human beings, unlike grains of a particular grade of wheat, are not fungible. Square pegs forced into round holes do not produce optimum results. In terms of money multiplication and compatibility, certain individual differences are of primary importance and they are rather easily identified.

Verbal skill is certainly one factor. Money multipliers usually have a strong command of their native language. They use words accurately and with respect. They are articulate, have relatively large, but not showy, vocabularies and their grammar and syntax are correct. They say what they mean and vice versa. As verbal skills are also a primary means of communication, this is an important compatibility consideration.

Logical and analytical thinking are also important in the multiplication of money. There exists in our society a cultural bias in favor of those able to manipulate words and numbers in logical, sequential order and these individuals are better able to create wealth in all industrialized societies as they are presently organized. The exception in this respect is in the arts and, although this is an important exception that should not be underestimated, artists comprise only a small segment of the population.

Another important factor that affects compatibility between and among people is whether or not they have the same dominant sense organ. Some people have a highly developed visual sense. Others have a keenly attuned sense of hearing. A musician and a painter, for example, may be equally sensitive and intelligent. However, a sonata, or even spoken words, will probably have greater impact on the former, whereas a beautiful sunset will probably affect the latter more deeply.

Unless those who are primarily visual or verbal are aware of these differences, they will not be communicating on the same wavelength. If, for example, you and another person are late to a dinner engagement or a business meeting, your verbal encouragements to hurry directed at a primarily visual person will have considerably less impact than your putting on of your hat and coat and heading for the door. Communication, to be meaningful, must find a receptive channel. Given a choice between posting a letter in a mailbox or the litter basket next to it, you would certainly choose the former in almost all cases.

There are scores of observable clues to organ dominance. Visual people tend to have about them visual objects of beauty, such as paintings, sculptures, beautiful furniture, and the like. They have a strong sense of color. They appreciate and react to their visible surroundings with greater sensitivity. They are picture-oriented. Verbal people have a strong sense of language, a highly developed feeling for words. Their surroundings tend to be more lean and bare, less lush. They are word-oriented; they usually own more books and probably pay higher telephone bills.

Other easily observable clues to compatibility include what the individuals find funny, whether or not they keep their commitments. Do they pay their bills on time? Are they punctual? Do they tend to procrastinate? Is their general view of the world similar to yours? Do they see the overview or concentrate on details? Are they enthusiastic, upbeat, or are they depressed? Are they flexible or inflexible, calm or volatile, mature or immature?

It is my contention that a greater regard to compatibility factors would facilitate communication, increase productivity, create greater happiness and well-being, multiply wealth and set in motion a vast train of additional beneficial consequences.

V

The Money Look

There is a continuous interaction between you and your total environment. Every element in your environment produces effects upon you and vice versa. The set of external elements over which you may be assumed to have choice and control and which are close and continuing parts of your life reflect, or mirror, your personality, your level of consciousness. What you choose or accept is a function and an extension of who you are. Confining this discussion to visual elements only, what you look like, what you wear, what's in your pockets or purse, what the inside and outside of your residences look like, the cars you drive and how you maintain them, your luggage, your houseplants and pets, your facial expressions, your hairstyle, your teeth, your skin, your silhouette, your posture, your carriage, your gestures, and, in fact, every element you choose or permit to become a close and continuing part of your visual presentation of yourself reflects, in some measure, your level of consciousness and is an index to your character and personality.

Moreover, the visual elements with which you are closely and regularly associated are part of your everyday visual field. They are continually sensed and fed back into your consciousness and become part of your self-image. Thus, the interaction loop is completed. Your consciousness is reflected in the visual choices you permit to become part of your daily life, and these choices, in turn, are sensed over and over again by you and become part of your consciousness. If, for example, in your living quarters or office, you surround yourself with an unsightly clutter of debris and detritus, it would not be unreasonable for others to conclude that you are an untidy person whose mind is needlessly cluttered, even if these conclusions are incorrect, in your judgment. These kinds of inferences are inescapable. In fact, if the overlay of rubbish piles up over a long enough period of time, it will modify even your own self-image.

The idea that how you think affects what you and your surroundings look like and how you and your surroundings look affect how you think is not novel. Significantly, this reciprocal relationship between your inner and outer environments provides an entry point for improvement in both environments through either. An improvement in your outer environment will produce a series of echoes that, in sum, will create a higher level of consciousness, and vice versa.

You may, for example, be familiar with a man or a woman who, having ended an unhappy love affair or marriage, has allowed his or her appearance, physical condition, and/or residence to become run-down, poorly maintained. These conditions gradually worsen, feeding upon the interaction loop described earlier, until a change is initiated from the inside out or from the outside in. Typically, the person becomes romantically involved with somebody else and this triggers a change in his or her appearance, physical condition and living quarters, or, the person sets about to change the look of the externals (goes on a strict diet, cleans up the place, etcetera), and this signals the real end of the unhappy love affair or marriage and a readiness for a serious romantic attachment.

There are many interesting applications of this phenomenon to the magic of thinking rich. Once you are ready to create important changes in your life by becoming wealthy, you would do well to take a fresh look at the sensory data with which you have been supplying yourself and realize how these data have been stored within you, ready to be fed back and confirm themselves in tangible, external circumstances. Once you are aware of the process and the specific bad data, each of the latter may be improved, eliminated or replaced. The theory behind this voluntary reprogramming is simple. Putting it into practice is up to you.

Most people receive the majority of their sensory data visually. "Seeing is believing." How things look create strong reactions. Predictable mood swings can be produced by changing the wall colors of a room. Behavior modification based on visual cues is an everyday fact of life. Even hyperactive children tend to lower their voices in a funeral chapel. Similarly, most people will refrain from littering an art museum or an immaculate garden, whereas when they walk into an already unkempt surrounding, they are less reluctant to add to the disorder.

In the same way, your visual presentation of yourself affects how other people receive you and react to you. Regardless of his intrinsic worthiness as a human being, would you be likely to seek out for financial consultation and guidance a man who arrives at your office or home to repair the wiring, carrying a toolbox, tools dangling from his belt, two ball-point pens clipped to his shirt pocket, the earpieces of his glasses held together by dirty adhesive tape, in paint-spattered shoes, and chewing gum?

As this sort of appearance fails to inspire confidence in connection with big-money dealings, so, too, does its opposite extreme. The man or woman who is overdressed in the latest fashions, overgroomed, and carrying too many shiny props reduces his or her chances for great financial success. Such extravagances are distasteful to wealthy people and arouse suspicion. Moneyed people are not among the first to wear the latest styles and often don't buy them at all, particularly if they are too highly stylized or exaggerated in any way. They tend to consider the latter wasteful, ostentatious, vulgar. There is a kind of reverse chic, among the old-moneyed, of wearing old clothing with old accessories and accouterments, although their quality and condition are likely to be first-rate. Women should be especially sensitive about being overdressed and groomed and carrying too many obviously new props lest they look like "overnight" successes of insufficient background and experience. In response to the special needs of women in business, a new kind of boutique has been created. Those interested in this approach would probably do well to call the magazine named for the largest city near where they live or work and ask for the names of these shops.

Have you noticed that almost everybody likes to "discover" relatively unknown show business talents and become their advocate and champion? Such discoverers take an almost proprietary interest in the success of their discoveries. This process usually continues and builds as the talent becomes recognized and established. However, if the talent becomes universally accepted, a superstar, his or her former admirers often become detractors, generously sharing their newly discovered evidence of clay feet.

In the same way, people are often reluctant to join forces with, or even help, somebody who simply talks about a money-making venture. However, if the individual actually sets about to advance the project in a serious, businesslike way and the project begins to move forward (as in the case of the relatively unknown talent who gets some gigs), some of the same people who were out to lunch before the project began to make any headway, are inclined to get on board.

This aspect of human behavior provides an insight into

the optimum "money look." The visual objective in attracting money-making opportunities and financial aid and support is to look as if you are "on the move" but not as if you have already arrived. There is a strong human impulse to avoid those whose needs are too great, to help those who are beginning to move forward, and to knock down the one who is already "king of the mountain."

In putting together a total look that will attract money and money-making opportunities, you must be as objective as possible. Look at yourself as would a director or a good casting director. As most people are startled the first time they listen to the sound of their recorded voice, they also have little idea of how they look. Nobody is likely to come up to you and tell you how ridiculous you look. We are much more likely to be told how well we look and to become lulled into believing it.

For little or nothing, in most big cities, you may have an opportunity to see yourself on videotape in color. For about the cost of a good dinner in a moderately priced restaurant, you may buy an hour's time with a professional coach. This will enable you to see yourself on videotape and to discuss how you may project a money look along the lines suggested here.

Television is the most pervasive communications medium in our society. Its signals penetrate virtually every household in the country an average of more than six hours each day. By virtue of this tremendous impact, there is a tendency for what works on television in terms of a money look to carry over into the society and to work in everyday life. An awareness of what does work in this medium will therefore be valuable.

As examples, I have selected four familiar television figures for study: Alistair Cooke, Ricardo Montalban, his brother Carlos, and John Houseman. All of these gentlemen except Mr. Cooke (who has turned down exceedingly handsome offers) is a spokesperson, and it is no accident that the product or service with which each is associated is an upscale one. Each is well cast in his role. Although each has an individual style different from all of the others, each has a distinctive money look of which the advertising industry seems to have taken notice. All of these television presentations are instructive.

Carlos Montalban, *El Exigente* (the Demanding One), of the long-running series of coffee commercials, established the characterization of a man of complete authority and the highest degree of specialized expertise without uttering a single word in the original series. We were, to be sure, cued by the voice-over, but the performance by Mr. Montalban was flawless and all of a piece. He walked "tall" with a confidence and sureness, an obvious pride in himself, but without hauteur. He had an intelligent, no-nonsense mien and, significantly, he wasted no words, a sign of power. He rejected carefully selected samples of coffee as not up to the standards of "the Demanding One." Then, encountering an example of coffee perfection that passed even his adamantine barriers, he bestowed his unqualified approval. The onlookers were relieved and delighted.

His portrayal, all accomplished without any lines, was remarkable. Perhaps a small point about the color of his suit should be clarified. Ordinarily, suits of dark colors command a certain authority in our society, whereas lighter colors make one more approachable. The choice of a light color for the Demanding One's suit may be attributed to the climate and social customs of the purported locale of the commercials. After a hiatus, *El Exigente* is back with us but, alas, he is no longer silent. Predictably, his verbal pitch reduces him and weakens his image.

Ricardo Montalban is a good choice to present a relatively high-priced automobile of domestic manufacture. Not only do Mr. Montalban's dignity and pride support this effort, but there is, I assume, an attempt to link the automobile's name with his family heritage. Mr. Montalban looks prosperous and attractive and his facial expressions and body movements are well synchronized with his speech. He seems to look directly at the viewer and to speak to each one of us personally, all of which add to his credibility and apparent interest in us.

There is, also, and perhaps not incidentally, something of a carry-over into the commercial of his starring portrayal in a long-running television series that adds to his effectiveness. He carries himself well; his movements are sure and unhurried, like those of a still well-conditioned former athlete. There is an understated, quiet elegance evident in the way he looks and this is underscored by his well-modulated delivery.

Although not a spokesperson for any product or service at this writing, Alistair Cooke certainly has had his share of offers, thus far all refused. As a host, Mr. Cooke presents himself as erudite and successful. The camera angle seems to be at eye level so that, although he is comfortably seated in a wing chair in a fairly opulent setting, the viewer does not look down on him (which might detract from his authoritativeness) but directly at him, for person-to-person communication. He appears to be talking to us, not reading lines off a TelePrompTer, a touch that adds to our admiration of his apparent storehouse of knowledge and depth of understanding and which creates a higher intensity of rapport. His is a controlled presence, correct and precise, spare of physical movement, gesture and language.

He is beautifully tailored in suits from Hawes and Curtis, outfitters of the Duke of Edinburgh. He speaks with an easy precision, rarely leaning on outside authority (which adds to his own personal importance), telling us his thoughts with a grand simplicity and without hedging. His posture, hairstyle, and all of the colors in the set, including those of his clothing, denote a refined taste, an opulence, a reservoir of wealth. He is also well-modulated, calm, unruffled and informed. He comes across the home screen not with some surface shine but with a deep, rich patina, an unmistakable money look.

John Houseman has been conspicuous in a series of television commercials for a securities brokerage company. The decision to associate Mr. Houseman with money management is felicitous. He projects an image of self-confidence only a few kilometers south of arrogance. He looks prosperous, well turned out, and the sets and locations are intended to resonate ease and elegance. There is also a carry-over of Mr. Houseman's award-winning performance in a motion picture and television series spin-off, in which he played a professor at a prestigious law school. This similarity of performance adds the weight of authority and professional accreditation of the law professor's persona to that of the brokerage-house spokesperson.

Mr. Houseman presents the image of a forceful, self-assured, intelligent man who is completely at home in the world of money and the alchemy of high finance. We know he had the energy and discipline to take on a starring role in a television series (which can make house-painting or hod-carrying seem like semi-retirement) at an age when many would be content to clip coupons and receive remittances in a sunny climate. He comes across as a man of the world, dominant, uncompromising, sure of himself and his opinions, an old pro in his well-cut, dark business suits, a man to whom even E. F. Hutton would pay heed.

Compare these four gentlemen, on the one hand, with two other spokespersons in terms of a money look. Frank Perdue is almost undoubtedly a man of substantial personal wealth. He is also a tall man, a natural asset for presenting men of distinction and power. Notice, for example, that all of the four gentlemen referred to earlier give the impression of height either naturally or through camera angles and the composition of the set. Great care is exercised in selecting and creating all of the sensory data of well-crafted commercials. Their production costs often exceed that of the program in which they are contained, and additional millions of dollars may be spent on the commercial time during which they are telecast.

Mr. Perdue, like Carlos Montalban, is advertising an item available in supermarkets. However, unlike the four men discussed earlier, he lacks a money look. This is by no means intended as a criticism of his effectiveness as a television spokesperson for his company. It may well be that Mr. Perdue is the best possible choice for the job. However, in terms of whether or not his presentation of himself would attract big money or large-scale, money-making opportunities in the real world outside the sets used in the production of the commercials, there are reasons to think not. Although we are told a number of times that his name and that of the company are the same, there is little visual evidence in his presentation to suggest any great distinction between Mr. Perdue and an assistant manager of one of the supermarkets that sells his company's products, with all due respect to Mr. Perdue and assistant managers of supermarkets as persons.

Phil Rizzuto, the former New York Yankee baseball star, is associated in television commercials with a finance company that makes loans of sums up to $50,000. He does not project a money look. His movements seem unnatural. The wardrobe is unimpressive and there is little presence in the performance. What we see is in the nature of another job of work, not a real identification with the sponsor's services. Significantly, both Mr. Perdue and Mr. Rizzuto also deliver their lines with a non-money sound. Mr. Perdue's voice is almost a whine, while Mr. Rizzuto's delivery is amplified in a way that separates him from the viewer's interest and promotes instant tuneout. The possibility that people who need to borrow money from a company like the one Mr. Rizzuto describes may find these commercials irresistible is, of course, entirely irrelevant to the consideration of whether Mr. Rizzuto, as he is presented in these commercials, does or does not have a money look.

Both Mr. Perdue and Mr. Rizzuto seem content to play themselves. Neither evidences interest in creating an image of success, of expertise, of ease and familiarity with large sums of money. This, despite the probability of Mr. Perdue's personal wealth and the fact that the subject of Mr. Rizzuto's sponsor's service is money itself. After the age of forty, one is said to get the face one deserves. The four faces described earlier are all strong. They give a sense of their own worth and dignity and an air of self-esteem. Not so the latter two. Mr. Rizzuto unconvincingly wastes motion and he shouts at us, italicizing every word and emphasizing none. Mr. Perdue comes at us in an undistinguished, plaintive singsong. There is no charisma, no leadership quality, no high style in the presentation. This lack of a money sound underscores the visual shortfall. That neither of these gentlemen is a trained actor misses the point, for most of the rest of us are not trained actors yet we may nevertheless be able to project a money look.

These examples were chosen from the television medium in order to provide familiar, highly identifiable presentations which were likely to have been seen in the past and which might be available for viewing in years to come. A money look is a composite, a total look. The elements that comprise it must be all of a piece, as discrepancies are jarring and all too apparent even to the untrained eye.

It would be foolish to wear a $200 pair of shoes with a $50 suit. The shoes, unfortunately, will be targeted by some and become a source of ridicule and scorn. Their wearer will be thought and said by some to be "putting on airs" and it will probably work against him or her at a time of greatest vulnerability. As was pointed out earlier, there is a mechanism that motivates people to support those who are on the move, to shun those who are simply making idle statements about the future, and to seek to topple those who are already "king of the mountain." The visual presentation that will attract the most and best money-making opportunities and discourage the fewest utilizes this mechanism. It presents the appearance of being about halfway to your goal and moving toward it, but not yet in possession of it.

If you have a field of interest, a focus for making money, become familiar with the look and style of the leaders in this field. If possible, personally visit the office buildings or other places in which they work, at their typical arrival times, lunchtimes and departure times. Get your own first-hand impressions. Find out when a convention or trade show will be in your city, or nearby, and visit it. Get a feeling for what successful people in your field look like, how they dress, walk, speak, what they drive, how they style their hair, etcetera. The details are important.

Color television can be a valuable resource. If you like what a local on-camera person looks like, call the station. With a little ingenuity and persistence you can find out who does his or her hair, where they shop, and so forth. There is a great difference between a first-rate hair stylist (or, indeed, a first-rate anything) and an average one and the former can create a style for you that will make a difference in your visual presentation of yourself for only a few extra dollars. Any competent professional may then easily copy it for you at the regular price. You can put the same top talent to work for you that created the hairstyle you like for the local television news, sports, weather, talk or game show person in almost every case. Be critical when you watch television. Decide whether what you see and hear reinforce one another or clash and cancel one another. Would you have cast this person in that role? Would you have dressed them differently or directed them differently?

In putting your wardrobe together, stay with the basics,

the classics, and avoid fads and exaggerated styles. You can buy a relatively inexpensive version of any basic look that suits you, especially if you wait for legitimate sales at reliable stores. Fit is important. Find out by telephone in advance who the head fitter is and whether that person will be there when you plan to shop. Ask for that person by name and be willing to tip for his or her help. Ask questions so you will learn all of the specifics of a good fit.

Accessories are an important part of your total look. Everything you buy should be considered as part of your entire wardrobe. Avoid obvious clashes and duplications in building this look. You can get help in any good store by asking for it. Find somebody who exhibits a style you like in the way he or she dresses and ask questions.

Correct all remedial physical liabilities. This money is well spent and pays dividends for life in a number of ways. If you have a skin condition and you permit it to persist it says something about you (over and over again) to yourself and others that will impede your progress en route to your own personal fortune. It may not be considered appropriate by some to mention this sort of thing but it is a fact that not everybody who sees you and makes decisions that affect your financial future is a philosopher. How you look makes a difference in the way you navigate toward wealth. In the real world, straight teeth are an asset and they encourage, and are part of, an attractive smile. Crooked teeth may not only create dental problems, they indicate a lack of care and self-esteem. On the other hand, if you are willing to pay the various costs in money, time and inconvenience to have your teeth straightened, others will also care more about you.

As you put together a total money look, you will find yourself developing momentum in seemingly unrelated areas. The world, or that part of the field of play on which you move, is an interrelated web controlled by mind. Your improved visual presentation will enhance your self-esteem, promote greater self-confidence. You will begin to think and feel better about yourself. It's something like the first time a person is promoted to the title of vice-president: soon, he or she is treated as a vice-president and begins to feel and act like a vice-president. You will develop this kind of feeling for yourself as you create your money look.

In the same way, as you surround yourself with possessions of quality and style and beauty and character, they will not only represent you more advantageously to the outside world, but they will also make you feel better about yourself from within. Items you have permitted to remain broken, frayed, or in disrepair will be mended or discarded and out of clutter will come order and orderliness, as the standards you set for yourself continue to rise.

Quality items that last a long time rise steadily in price, sometimes dramatically. Fountain pens I began to buy for about forty dollars now sell for about three hundred dollars (if you can find them) and have become collector's items since their manufacturer discontinued that particular model in favor of an inferior copy now retailing for about $175. Good clothes, particularly if they are imported, have also soared in price.

Develop a style that works for you, one that is appropriate to your size, build, coloring, age and to your objectives. If the financial goal you have in mind is not within easy reach, be prepared to create your visual presentation in two stages. Don't present a partial look by acquiring one or two expensive items which you plan to wear with your old wardrobe because you can't afford a total look at the moment. As was pointed out above, this will tend to encourage unnecessary sniping by some who will be made uncomfortable by your attempts to improve your position.

Take your time. Plan, think, observe, learn, do the research. Get into good physical shape. Get your finances under control. Find a hairstyle. Watch for sales of what you want. Learn the prices and how they change. Visualize how each item will fit into your total look. Transfer at least one of your accounts to the most prestigious bank in your community. Get at least one high-prestige credit card. These items are part of a total visual presentation. Begin to stockpile the components of your new look. Above all, don't discuss these plans before, during, or after your execution of them. You would be inviting criticism and would dissipate a great deal of the energy and impetus to follow through. Upgrade everything you carry in your pockets or purse. Get some good luggage. Find a cologne that suits you. As you begin to look and act and move and feel as if you're already halfway to your financial goal, you will become more attractive to money and money-making opportunities. Soon, others will begin to think of you as "lucky" and you will be well on your way.

VI

Money Talk

Words have magical properties of which many people have been aware for centuries with varying degrees of sophistication. In the Middle Ages, for example, individuals were loath to give their names to others because they believed that if somebody knew their name, he or she could exercise some measure of control over them. You create with words countless linguistic thought patterns that are either expressed as speech or are simply communicated to yourself (and anybody else who may be able to deduce, intuit or divine them) in the form of unvoiced thoughts. In an earlier chapter, I stated my conviction that these thousands and thousands of spoken and unspoken communications are of enormous importance in determining your life-style. They are characteristic of you; their style is your style. What you say to yourself and to others is a major determinant of your life.

The effects of what you say to yourself were examined at some length earlier; the effects of what you say to others was deferred until now. The human voice is a wondrous instrument. It is able to communicate the inconsolable anguish of a child suddenly bereft. It caresses the ear and the heart with a love song or a sonnet. It soothes, it orders, it chides and insinuates. Orotund oratory, philosophical discourses and theological exegeses are all within its compass.

In addition, and of special significance to the magic of thinking rich, what you say and how you say it will play an important role in making you wealthy. Among our earliest human ancestors, some were better able than others to use primitive cries and grunts to communicate danger and the locations of potential food supplies. Those so gifted no doubt improved the chances of survival of their immediate group and probably earned the most coveted rewards.

The process of transforming vocal skills into personal rewards and distinctions has never ceased. In fact, the opportunities for turning ordinary words into wealth are more abundantly available now than ever before. It is this magic we will be exploring, a process even more wonderful than that which animated the hopes and dreams of ancient alchemists. You have the ability to transform what and how you communicate with others and thereby to transform your entire life.

One of the effects of the extension of communication via the enormous penetration of the electronic media in our society is the displacement of the printed and written word by the spoken word. Verbal communication is not only crucial in entertainment and the arts, government and industry, business, the military and the professions, it is the foundation on which virtually *all* relationships are built. As never before, the primary element in your daily presentation of yourself is the spoken word. These everyday voiced exchanges provide the contextual environment of your relationships much as the atmosphere supplies the contextual environment for the support of your life. How you express yourself in speech provides an index to your character, colors your past, creates your present and determines your future.

Elocution, speech etiquette, the production of pear-shaped tones, perfect diction, impeccable grammar, a scholarly vocabulary, and a number of other elements usually accorded great emphasis are almost completely irrelevant, and will, in fact, often be counterproductive to the use of speech as a means of making you rich. Many people of good will, for example, would probably consider bravura performances and showy demonstrations of proficiency in these technical skills reasonable grounds for social ostracism.

Our concern is with creating a context in which to relate to other people from the sheer gossamer of speech—a beautifully resilient springboard from which you may launch your life in any direction that pleases you and by which you may attract into your life all the money you want. You may look upon what you say as a valuable medium of exchange, a renewable, refinable resource, a treasure trove, yours, with a little effort and knowledge, to be claimed whenever you decide to do so.

We will focus our attention not on the mechanics of speech, although they will not be ignored, but on the dynamics of the medium of speech, the best methods of presenting yourself attractively and effectively, the ways to reduce the separations between yourself and other human beings with whom you chance or choose to interact, so that you may reach mutual respect and affection, support and common purpose. This is an entirely different undertaking from the achievement of technical proficiency in speech. The latter is almost collateral to our purpose for the same reason that a champion checker player would find his or her skills unavailing in a chess match. While the field of play, that is, the board (or speech) is the same in both cases, the objectives and the rules of the games are completely different.

It is much easier to enlist and enroll the people you meet so that they help you than it is to approach each person as

somebody who must be skewered, steamrollered or fi-
nessed. It is, after all, through cooperation, rather than
conflict, that your greatest successes will be derived, for
bad vibes are unmistakable and their results are highly
predictable, if self-defeating. In approaching life as conflict, you may win a few inconsequential skirmishes but
you will be sowing the seeds for your ultimate unfulfillment. That orientation may enable you to stumble, or even
walk, through life but it cannot help you dance or fly.

Many have become sophisticated "body language" as
well as speech interpreters and can "read" the subtext, the
vibe, the very psyche of the speaker or the observed subject, with or without mechanical crosscheck. A competent
actor can get fifty different line readings out of as simple a
phrase as "Next week," and we, the audience, are able to
understand the various shades of meanings. The written
or printed word is also capable of communicating
thoughts and feelings but it gives rise to a more solitary
occupation and produces, as Marshall McLuhan has often
observed, separation, specialization and fragmentation. A
broader, cruder gauge, print is simply incapable of this
degree of subtlety.

While the ability to interpret the vibes of others is undoubtedly of some value, of far greater importance and
largely unremarked, is the ability to create excellent,
money-attracting vibes of your own, for this latter ability
contains within it the potential to transform your life. Instead of learning how best to report the weather, or even
to produce it, would it not be more to the point to learn
how to create for yourself a climate in which you may
flourish? Why attempt to throw a pile of bricks into the air
in the hope they will fall in a useful arrangement when
you can design a Taj Mahal, a house in the country, a
factory or a university and be reasonably certain it will be
built as conceived and planned from the foundation up,
inside and out?

More than any other element, it is what you say and how

you say it that determines who you are (your identity), where you are (your status), where you're coming from (your background), and where you are going (your direction). If character is destiny, how you express yourself in speech provides an index to your character. Mastery of the art of money talk requires a certain proficiency in the use of the language tools, sensitivity to interpersonal cues and the ability to respond most effectively to them.

As you do not see yourself as others see you (you see a mirror image subjectively), you do not hear yourself as others hear you. You listen to yourself from the inside; others listen to you from the outside. Your bones and cavities conduct the sound of your voice and you are much more affected by this than the other listeners who hear your speech via air conduction. You are, in effect, behind your own voice, listening to it as it leaves you. Others normally hear your voice as it comes toward them. You also hear your voice at extremely close range, producing an additional distortion others don't perceive. Most people are surprised, if not shocked, to hear their normal speaking voices faithfully recorded. However, despite this initial unfamiliarity, you nevertheless have a characteristic sound of your own. Your voiceprint is as much a part of your identity as your fingerprint; even more so, for your voiceprint includes a large psychological, as well as physical, component.

Professional speech therapy is available to you if you need and want it. So, too, is vocal coaching if that is indicated. However, as a first step toward a deeper understanding and appreciation of the wonderful instrument you may have been neglecting, I would respectfully suggest you might profit from some books any good dramatic school, the drama department of a college or university, or a public library may supply on this subject. With a little effort you can reverse the effects of years of neglect, if such is the case.

Good voice production of standard or regional speech (if

the latter is otherwise correct and does not interfere with comprehension) is necessary, but not sufficient, for money talk. In addition, proper diction, grammar and usage will give a strong spine of authority to what you say. Your money talk repertoire should also include a large, although not showy, vocabulary. Decades of testing of hundreds of thousands of people comprising a broad cross section of the United States population indicates that vocabulary bears the highest correlation with success and achievement of any measurable variable. As not only what you say, but so much of what you think, consists of words, it would be difficult to imagine great articulation, subtlety and breadth of thought without a correspondingly large vocabulary. The proposition that vocabulary and not education is the key correlate with success and achievement has been suggested by testing high school dropouts. When compared with executives who were college graduates, the best scores of the high school dropouts who attained major executive positions were equal.

Acquiring a large vocabulary is easy but it requires a systematic approach. You learn words in a progression of levels. As in constructing a skyscraper, each floor is built, in turn, from the foundation to the roof. Therefore, simply learning this or that word will not suffice. You must begin at your present level and improve successively. Learning a dozen new words will then give you an understanding of several times that number so progress can be rapid, especially so below the highest levels.

Thirty Days to a More Powerful Vocabulary by Wilfred Funk and Norman Lewis, the latter's *Word Power Made Easy* and Johnson O'Connor's *English Vocabulary Builder* should serve you well in this context. Money talk also requires that you have a firm grasp of the grammar and usage of your native language. H. W. Fowler has written a couple of useful books in this connection or you may wish to consult a good librarian for other suggestions. A spare amount of time and effort spent in this way will easily change any false notes you may be sounding into the grace notes of proper expression.

Once you achieve the firm foundation of good voice production, acceptable diction, a powerful vocabulary and a sure command of grammar and usage, you are ready for the refinements of money talk, the specific techniques by which to use these tools to convert what you say and how you say it, to cash. You may have noticed that the various elements of the magic or thinking rich are compatible with, and support, one another. These elements work most effectively in combination, in concert.

To attract money and money-making opportunities to you what you say should present you as a source not a conduit. Therefore, do not cite sources of authority or the agreement of others with respect to your statements or points of view. If others may easily go to your source, they may finesse you. This cancels you as both a power source and a toll point, a basic error. In addition, to rely on outside sources is a sign of weakness.

Do not discuss hopes or future plans that are, or may be, beyond your control. The less said about the future the better as future events are often unpredictable. Do not overstate or exaggerate. Do not hedge or qualify; state or wait. Speak clearly and loudly enough to be heard but don't raise your voice unnecessarily. Don't repeat or explain anything unless asked to do so. Never define yourself or describe yourself as the kind of person who never (or always) does (or doesn't do) this or that. The moment you define yourself, you limit yourself (by definition).

When you speak of a project that interests you or that might become a cooperative venture with the person with whom you're speaking, approach it from the point of view of what you intend to accomplish, not how much money you hope or expect to make. Be enthusiastic but not extravagant. Do not give your word lightly. Once given, however, you are obligated to keep your commitment. In doing so, put as good a face on it as you can muster, lest bad grace nullify good actions.

Never belittle or criticize yourself verbally. If others are argumentative or difficult, don't become embroiled in a verbal duel or slugfest. In may be helpful, for future reference, if you can discover whether there is something you are presenting that triggered this reponse. Don't impart information idly and don't gossip. Keep the confidences of others and don't reveal your own secrets to gain easy rapport.

A simple money talk technique involves the speed at which you speak. Contrary to the popular stereotype of the fast-talking pitchman, as James Maclachlan points out in "What People Really Think of Fast Talkers" in the November, 1979, issue of *Psychology Today*, the experimental data consistently show fast talkers (180–200 words per minute) are more persuasive, and seem more knowledgeable and intelligent than average-speed talkers (140–160 words per minute) and slow talkers (100–120 words per minute). Fast talkers also come across as more to be trusted, more sincere and more interesting. Most people prefer to hear speech at a rate about 25 percent faster than average and this in no way impairs the comprehension of standard speech. Fast speech also focuses more attention on what is said, as listeners are usually more attentive and less likely to interrupt.

If a poker player were able to correctly "read" every other player at the table, you would expect most of the chips to gravitate toward him or her. The proponents of "Neurolinguistic Programming" (NLP), a linguist named John Grinder and Richard Bandler, a Gestalt therapist, have been training doctors, lawyers, sales personnel and others to obtain certain results through communication, the creation of a high degree of rapport and other techniques. There are some applications of these methods to money talk.

In *The Structure of Magic II* (Science and Behavior Books, Inc., Palo Alto, California), Messrs. Bandler and Grinder set forth their fascinating approach. Although you sense the world through several organs, the primary and most direct way you have to communicate your sense of the world is through language. In doing so, you reveal a great deal of material about yourself, much of which without your awareness. One of the objectives of money talk is to increase your conscious awareness of what you say, how you say it and its effects upon others so that you can exercise greater control over your conversations. Another objective is to indicate how you can learn to speak in ways that expand and multiply options without reducing any, so that your field of action is broadened. NLP offers a way of establishing a high degree of rapport fairly easily. In sum, the objective is to broaden, deepen and magnify your personal language power.

By paying attention to which of the major input channels (sight, hearing or kinesthetics) a speaker favors in the language selected to express his or her thoughts and feelings, you may identify the speaker's "primary representational system," to use Bandler and Grinder's terminology. By responding to the speaker in the same mode, via the same input channel, the speaker is made to feel better understood, more en rapport. For example, suppose a speaker, whose "primary representational system" was kinesthetic (body sensations) asked: "How do you *feel* about that?" A response such as: "I don't like the *sound* of it," or "It *looks* bad," would not be as appropriate for establishing closeness and trust as: "It makes me feel terrible," or "I feel sick about it."

As "speaking the same language" enhances a relationship of trust and rapport and understanding, approaching another on the "wrong" wavelength, that is, through other than their "primary representational system," interrupts the flow. This awareness of the other person's primary representational system and the making of attempts to communicate via this input channel gives you another communications strategy and improves your skill and effectiveness in reaching others; i.e., it facilitates your "getting through" to more people.

In *Frogs into Princes,* a fascinating and magical book edited from audiotapes of NLP training workshops conducted by Bandler and Grinder, they posit a link between a person's eye movements and his or her specific sensory processing. In a "normally organized" right-handed person, upward eye movements indicate the individual is thinking about visual images. Upward and to the right indicates the visual image is one they haven't seen before but are creating or constructing; upward and to the left indicates a remembered visual image. Defocused and unmoving eyes also indicate visual imagery.

In the same person, eye movements directly to the right means thought about a sound not heard before; eye movements directly to the left denote thinking about a remembered sound and eye movements down and to the left indicate a kind of talking to oneself. Finally, in this schematic way, in the same person, eye movements down and to the right provide a clue to kinesthetic feelings and (less importantly) smell and taste sensations. By becoming aware of another's characteristic eye movements, you may learn how the person accesses information. Your speaking to people through their favored sensory channel gives you more direct access to them and establishes a closer relationship and greater understanding and rapport.

What not to say is an important part of money talk. Requests for information should be used sparingly. They tend to make the questioned person more important than the questioner. Don't preface such inquiries with a long introduction or explanation as to why you want or need this information and don't ask for permission for asking: "Let me ask you this . . ." This is weak. A simple "Why?" with a smile is a much stronger expression and the smile eliminates the hostility that might be inferred. Do not compare your financial progress, whether favorably or unfavorably, with that of anybody else. Never second-guess yourself or point to this or that opportunity missed or ignored. Do not discuss financial deals or dealings with people not involved in them or intimately involved with you. In any such discussions, omit some of the connecting links. You are not in education. If that's what you think your function is, become a teacher. If you want to be rich, educate yourself to the golden value of silence, a multipurpose tool. Silence includes not revealing the mechanics of deals, not claiming credit for yourself, not automatically responding informatively to all questions and not bad-mouthing others. Leave the "who, what, why, where and when" to the journalists and don't permit yourself to become an interviewee of anybody who happens to have some idle (or pointed) questions to ask. Stop the outflow.

In telephone conversations, don't be perfunctory. Picture in your mind the person with whom you are speaking. Pay more, not less, attention to both sides of the conversation than you would if you were speaking face-to-face. You have no visual cues so you must be especially attentive to what you hear. Don't try to do two things at once or anything extrinsic to the conversation that divides your interest. Interrupt as infrequently as possible and keep your energy level up. Try to maintain an imaginary eye contact.

Become aware of the way people present themselves. Courtrooms are instructive if you can find the time. Lawyers, judges, witnesses, parties, the staff, spectators all provide visual and verbal cues. What is it about their utterances and their manner that you like or dislike? Do they have a money sound? Is their sound consistent with their visual presentation of themselves? What helpful advice could you give them? Tape-record your side of several telephone conversations and ask yourself similar questions.

A money sound originates from its own, self-contained power source. Don't solicit agreement or confirmation. ("Am I right? Wouldn't you agree?") Don't "buttress" your statements with the accord or approval of others: "Herb and I wanted you to know . . ." Edit out the "I think" and "In my opinion . . ." Avoid collecting and passing on a stream of anecdotes whose points are that the world is a place of death, disease, injustice, hardship and other woes of all descriptions, over which people have little or no control. Take surprising news without expressing shock. Don't express continual and easy agreement and affirmation. Withhold it often enough so that your agreement and affirmation are not taken for granted.

In soliciting help of any kind, which should be done sparingly, phrase the request in a way that makes it easier for the other person to grant it. Not "You don't have change of a dollar, do you?" but "Are you able to change this?" holding out a fairly clean single, will get your change a lot more often. The form of the request is important. "Take my hand" will get the result you want more often than "Give me your hand." A different name for what you want can get the result for you if you use your imagination. For example, calling the result desired "a scholarship" instead of permission to take a course without paying anything makes it easier for the person who has the authority to grant the request to do so. The more specifications and details you load into a request, the less likely you are to get help. If you ask for a 16½-ounce ball-peen hammer with a shock-absorbent grip, etcetera, you obviously make it harder for the other person to give you a hammer that would do the job as well.

A conversation is not a contest to be won or lost or a field of battle on which to subdue the other side. It is an opportunity to exchange thoughts and feelings. Money talk involves the sharpening of a number of useful tools that may profitably be included among the other tools of language. The more choices, the more flexibility, the more strategies you can muster, the more skillful and successful you will be at converting opportunities to realities. Skillful money talk creates solid opportunities for converting talk to money.

VII

Money Talismans

In the World War II Hollywood army movies, there was a familiar character much chided by his buddies for his belief in his good luck charm. Later, this character would suddenly become aware that his lucky charm, or talisman, had gotten lost and become upset. In the next encounter with the enemy, he would be killed and his formerly scoffing buddies would be properly contrite.

The Oxford English Dictionary states, as its first definition of the word "talisman," "a stone, ring, or other object engraven with figures or characters, to which are attributed the occult powers of the planetary influences and celestial configurations under which it was made; usually worn as an amulet to avert evil from or bring fortune to the wearer; also medicinally used to impart healing virtue; hence, any object held to be endowed with magic virtue; a charm." With specific reference to "any object held to be endowed with magic virtue; a charm," it is the burden of this chapter of *The Magic of Thinking Rich* to explicate how you may devise a money talisman for yourself and endow it with magical virtue so that it brings fortune to its wearer.

Talismans have numerous qualities and functions. Put-

ting aside for the moment any consideration of the super-
natural attributes or occult powers of talismans, and
planting our feet firmly in the natural world of sensory
data, there are a number of ways in which they may nevertheless be useful. We may agree, for example, that a money
talisman provides a convenient, portable, three-dimen-
sional, concrete focus for galvanizing goal-directed
thoughts into productive action. The talisman serves to
add to the power of the mental processes involved a load
of sensory data and a tangible form. For example, assume
that you would like to own a second home, but for whatever combination of reasons, you have not yet acquired
such a property. In the course of time, this desire might
ordinarily tend to become intermittent and wane. It would
shift outside of your focus of attention, occasionally flit-
ting into your consciousness at increasingly greater intervals.

Suppose, however, that you now decide to use a money
talisman in order to help bring about your ownership of a
second home. If what you desire is an *actual* second home,
as opposed to the idea or thought or concept of your own-
ing a second home, you must become activated. That is to
say, you must set about the doing of what you want to
accomplish. In this case, that would involve setting forth
in writing all of the particulars of the home you want to
own as specifically as possible (at the same time being
aware that this list will be modified in accordance with
your actual findings). You would then go shopping in the
real world of second homes for the size, acreage, type,
price range, and in the locations you have particularized.
Anybody seriously in the market for such a property
would probably communicate with brokers in the locations specified and go out to look at the most likely possibilities. Evey time you did so you would be adding data,
through every sensory channel, to the mere thought of acquiring such a property.

The thought of acquiring a second home would thus be given some shape and definition. You would have begun to match your written outline of what you wanted with what is currently available, probably adjusting your preconceptions to the realities of the marketplace. You would have met with brokers and owners, visited actual sites, and you would have become additionally informed by sensing masses of data. All of these actions would tend to create an impetus, a momentum, that would serve to drive the project forward, presumably culminating in good title.

The mechanism of the talisman adds another dimension. By definition, the talisman, or charm, for bringing about your acquisition of a second home may be "any object" but you should select the most appropriate object for producing this specific result. A lightweight object, easily carried about in your pocket or purse (or worn as jewelry) and one that would continually remind you of this specific goal would be a good starting point. The object should, ideally, have some special significance in your mind that links it to the objective. A small stone found in the area of your choice, a souvenir purchased in a local gift shop, a locket containing a small quantity of local flora, or any of scores of other portable objects would serve provided it were carefully selected for its special significance to you. It must be a personal choice after careful thought.

It is important your talisman be sensed not as a stone, a souvenir, some local flora in a locket, or whatever it might otherwise be. It must be looked upon as a means of facilitating your obtaining what you, in good conscience, desire. It must bring to mind precisely what you want in all of its sharp, clear and special details. These details are not only visual; they include all of your senses. The more reality with which you invest your talisman, the more potent its effects.

The talisman's portability facilitates its entering your consciousness but you should not permit its familiarity to erode its magic or its symbology. Each time you become aware of your talisman you should allow its associative sensory data to flood into your consciousness and suffuse you. This will help you become more finely attuned to information in your environment that will, in turn, take you closer to your goal. Some of this information might otherwise escape notice.

If it is a sum of money you wish, determine exactly how much that sum is. Focus on what you will do with this sum. Let the details sink into your mind. Get the feeling of this wealth and all it will mean to you and any others close to you who will share in its benefits. Create as much sensory detail as you can. Let all of your senses have free rein in supplying these details. Soak in all of the sensory data. Bask in them.

After you decide what you will buy with some of this money, go out and actually look at these items. If it's a specific automobile, go to an auto show or to the showroom. Touch the car you want. Sit in it. Get the feel and the smell of the new leather in your mind so you may recall it at will. Look at the various parts of the car. Study the details. Sit at the wheel. Picture yourself sitting at the wheel. Transform this constructed image into an eidetic image. Listen to the sound as you open and close the doors. Honk the horn. Don't be shy about it. It's only a reproducible machine. You are a marvelous, unique, irreplaceable human being, and the scale of your value is incomparable with that of any material thing. You are worthy of the best that money can buy. Feel wealthy and in possession of all of the things you will buy. Feel good about yourself and make these feelings as real as you can.

Think of a talisman you can carry about as a means of focusing on the sum of money you selected as your goal. A special, old coin? Perhaps an original photograph of a particular person of great wealth and character you find congenial? Perhaps an autograph of this person, which you may be able to buy for a few dollars, or a signed letter? In suggesting possible talismans, you may have noticed that I've mentioned items that might have associations or influences that would combine with the sensory data. If, for example, you want to acquire a second home, or a large sum of money, you might have selected some game elements, such as a little green house or a $500 bill from a Monopoly set. These game elements would serve well as useful reminders of a goal and provide a focal point into which you could concentrate a great deal of sensory data for easy access. They would strengthen your resolve, help get you into an active mode and moving toward your goal. They would also affect your expectations, which, in turn, would affect results.

All very positive and beneficial, but so far these benefits are within the realm of science. The placebo effect, the halo effect, momentum, focus, sensory data, concretizing a specific goal, etcetera, these phenomena are all familiar and there is widespread agreement, anecdotal evidence and experimental data in support of their efficacy, all of which are recognized by the conventional sciences. No special magic here so far.

May we now raise the ante? Would you be willing to suspend disbelief as we explore, as promised earlier, how you may devise for yourself a money talisman endowed with magical virtue so that it brings fortune to its wearer? The magic referred to in this context is outside the current realm of the scientific establishment, although the latter is aware of what may be called energy exchanges. Some contend that the human body is a kind of storage battery and that through the transfer, by contact, of a surplus of energy from one person's body to that of another who has a deficiency in this "life-force," healings may be effected. It may be that the healings reportedly attributed to "the laying on of hands" are the results of such transfers.

A wide variety of experiments have attempted to test the hypothesis of energy transfers. In a series of tests known as "the tomato experiments," one tomato was placed in a glass of "energized" tap water and another was placed in a glass of ordinary tap water. Both tomatoes remained in their respective glasses of water overnight, after which each was placed on a plate and exposed to the indoor atmosphere. Within three days, the tomato that had been in the glass of water containing ordinary tap water began to leak and its condition deteriorated steadily. The tomato previously exposed to the energized tap water developed a small leak after eight days, which subsequently "healed," and it continued to maintain itself for a period of three weeks.

At McGill University, water "energized" by "psychic healers" was given to plants. Their growth rate was significantly greater than that of plants in a control group. Other experiments have been conducted that support the conclusion that energy purportedly imparted to a wide range of food items seems to retard their spoilage for extended periods of time.

Energy transfers involving physical contact have been measured and photographed. Kirlian photography indicates both the presence and the transference of what appears to be an energy field. Some believe that energy may be transferred without physical contact and that this transference can be affected at great distances by the force of mind, or thought, waves.

There appears to be some support for this belief. Consider the ability of a bloodhound to "pick up the scent" of an individual and to track and locate this person over time and distance by sniffing an item or items of property belonging to the person and then, presumably, following the trail of this scent. Human trackers are also capable of uncanny feats of detection in picking up trails and in locating missing persons on the scantiest of evidence. These accomplishments may be explained on the basis of ordinary physical, sensory data.

A rather different phenomenon, however, involves the

obtaining of, for want of a better term, what might be called "information" by touching or holding various objects. There are, for example, individuals who are able to hold or touch items of personal property belonging to, say, a missing person, and to state with great precision and detail where the missing person is, whether he or she is alive or dead, often accompanied by accounts of how and why they came to be "missing." Such "psychometrists" have worked, and are working, with various local police departments and their special powers are well documented.

How is such a feat possible? One theory posits some residual material that remains attached to tangible objects, or even lingers evanescently in the vicinity after an individual has left. By going into an altered state of consciousness, those gifted in this way can somehow hone in on this residue and pick up sensory data concerning the past and present activities of the person from whom the residual material emanated, through apparently extrasensory means.

In a January 29, 1980, New York Times article, Malcolm W. Browne quotes Dr. Brian Josephson, 1973 Nobel prize winner in physics, as being "99 percent convinced" of the reality of certain paranormal effects including "remote viewing" and mental metal bending. Says Dr. Josephson: ". . . physical law itself may have to be redefined in terms of some new principles. It may be that some effects in parapsychology are ordered-state effects of a kind not yet encompassed by physical theory. My interest is not only in parapsychology but in the nature of intelligence and consciousness. These are also ordered processes which are not yet understood. . . . It may be that an understanding of intelligence and consciousness lies outside the paradigm of physics. It may be that more can be learned about the nature of reality through meditative processes."

The magical effects talismans exert may somehow operate through the residual material attached to them. This material may have been implanted intentionally in the talisman by a "magician" or it may simply reside in or on the talisman by virtue of its contact with one or more former owners. Perhaps relics are much sought after and prized for some of these reasons. It is within this ineffable residual stuff the earlier imparted magic may inhere, later to become activated and to avert evil or bring fortune to its new wearer. The magic of the talisman is strengthened on physical contact in a proper state of mind and a congeries of desire, belief and expectancy.

As talismans fashioned for your special benefit by a powerful magician are not ordinarily available, an alternative means of securing such a charm must be found. An item of property in actual contact with a person whose accomplishments and temperament you find attractive and would consider a suitably instructive model, at least in these terms, may well have stored within it sufficient talismanically magical stuff to avert evil from, and bring fortune to, you. These results might be enhanced if your talisman were regularly placed in direct physical contact with you while you were in a proper state of mind and accompanied by your strong feelings of desire, belief and expectancy.

In order to select the person whose "magic" will thus be transmitted talismanically for your benefit, some thought and study are suggested. If you are not personally acquainted with such a candidate, you may be able to find published accounts of the persons you are considering for your own talismanic magician written by those who knew him or her personally as well as by others. In addition, for a more rounded insight and a different perspective you may be able to discover original published and/or unpublished writings and/or other products of your prospective magician's mind. It is helpful to be able to feel a closeness with this person.

After you have selected your magician, you will need to consider how to obtain a suitable talisman. If the person is or was somebody of your acquaintance, you may already possess something that had been in physical contact with him or her that might serve this function. If not, you may be able to obtain some item of personal property of no great monetary value. If the person were famous but not of your acquaintance, autographs, signed letters or small items of memorabilia are usually available through dealers at a fairly modest price.

For example, the great industrialist and philanthropist Andrew Carnegie died in 1919. Mr. Carnegie gave away about $400,000,000. Some of his beneficence was used to establish Carnegie Hall in New York, the Carnegie Institute of Washington, the Carnegie Hero Fund Commission, the Carnegie Foundation for the Advancement of Teaching, the Carnegie Endowment for International Peace, and about 3,000 libraries. In The Gospel of Wealth, he sets forth his conviction that wealthy people are "trustees" of their surplus wealth and should administer their riches for the public good. This great man's autographs are currently available for about ten dollars and signed letters and programs of his may be purchased for a somewhat higher, two-digit number of dollars. Dealers in these items are rather good about referring prospective buyers to colleagues in other cities if they are out of stock.

The entertainment industry is probably the best example of a realm in which an individual can rise from the ranks of the unemployed to a six- or seven- (sometimes eight-) figure paycheck with dizzying speed. Even taking into account the years of preparation that might have gone into the mix and the lean years, the rewards for the successful can be stupendous. Ten-million-dollar record and two- and three-million-dollar movie contracts are not unknown. Although these are so far the exception, smaller, though substantial, sums are by no means unusual for a few weeks' work. Perhaps there is some connection between this scale of income and the widespread belief in (and practice of) magic in the entertainment world.

Talismanic magic, coupled with a strong desire, belief and expectancy and a properly prepared mental state can produce personal miracles. José Silva, founder of Silva Mind Control, considers desire, belief and expectancy the "basic factors of programming." It is not enough, according to Mr. Silva, that we get ideas, transform them into images, and then expect the brain automatically to bring them into being. We must have a strong desire for what we program and we must believe and expect to realize the desired results. "Without these factors our programming becomes lifeless and void of meaning, for the brain is a living computer and responds to living programs. Our programs only become alive when they have value in our eyes, and when we believe the outcome will materialize."

In order to strengthen the powers of your talisman, you should become attuned to, en rapport with, your magician. As pointed out earlier, a study of the life of your magician through biography and autobiography and other writings, if available, is helpful in this connection. Absorb the details. Written notes should be taken and kept. Understand the thinking of your magician and develop a sympathetic state of mind. If convenient, visit some of the homes and other sites associated with this man or woman. Remember to take your talisman with you.

As you read and visit and reflect, open your mind to how these new data are affecting your thoughts and feelings. Anchor these thoughts and feelings through physical contact with your talisman, so that subsequent contacts with your talisman will readily call them forth. In the same way, anchor the strong imagery of your specific goals to your talisman.

When you look at your talisman and hold it in your hand, you should feel the calm that comes with a new understanding and appreciation of your own self-worth and a recognition of your own inherent potentials.The powers of your talismanic magician will be working for you and supporting you in the accomplishment of the goal you have set for yourself and in the accomplishment of future goals to be set in the same way.

Stoke the fires of your imagination with positive impressions worthy of your best efforts and feel free to "dream big." Feel the power and the magic of thinking rich. Nobody succeeds beyond his or her wildest expectations unless he or she begins with some wild expectations. Expectations alone, however, will not produce the desired results. You must be willing to take an active, principled approach to the living of your life and the attainments you set for yourself. It is then that your money talisman, anchored with your creative thoughts and feelings and the strong imagery of your goals, will work its magic.

VIII

The Magic of Trading Up

"Trading in" and "trading up" are familiar concepts. The family car, for example, used to be "traded in" at regular intervals. The process involved selling the old car to the dealer and using the proceeds as partial payment for the new one. As credit became more readily available, the practice of "trading up" replaced "trading in." This refinement allowed the owner of the old car to use the proceeds of its sale as a down payment on a more expensive make or model. Thus, the old car was not merely replaced with a similar one of a later vintage, but with a "better" one. This concept of trading up has many applications. For example, in employment, people will get promotions or switch jobs and/or companies as a means of improving their positions. However, there is no magic in these kinds of transactions.

These non-magical examples of trading up are usually guided by the principles of more, better and/or faster. As a means of increasing profitability, for example, companies continually strive to produce and sell *more* of whatever it is, or seek to turn out a *better* product, the new and improved item, or they will contrive to provide the desired result *faster*. More, better and faster are also the usual means by which those who work for a living rise in the corporate hierarchy, private practitioners and other individuals increase their billing rates, and otherwise improve their respective bottom lines. They are, perhaps, acceptable means for doing better but they are by no means exceptional. More, better and faster produces only additive increments. They function by accretion over time in a continuum. They tend to provide one-rung-at-a-time corporate ladder ascents and other limited, measured advances. In a previous chapter, some of the applications of this sort of leverage were considered.

For those willing to take a more venturesome approach, the rewards of magic are far greater. Magic is not an additive process. Magic is discontinuous, discrete, exponential, transformational. To illustrate the difference between magic and the non-magic of more, better and faster, here are a couple of examples.

There's a store in New York City that sells chocolate for eighteen dollars a pound. You can buy all the chocolate you can eat for three or five dollars a pound in New York City but if you want the finest Swiss chocolate and you're in New York, you pay the eighteen dollar-a-pound price or you don't get it. That's admittedly a high price for chocolate but, curiously, many who pay it happily would be outraged if somebody tried to sell them two- or three- or even five-dollar-a-pound chocolate for, say, eight dollars. The best (which is even better than better) commands its own price and you either pay it or you don't get the best.

Mechanical inventions and innovative processes also give us more, better and faster but the differences are essentially quantitative, not qualitative. Even "better," an apparently qualitative comparison, is applied quantitatively; i.e., better in reality means better by a certain, usually rather small, quantitative margin or difference, not so greatly different quantitatively that it becomes essentially different qualitatively. It refers, in this way, to a difference in degree, not in kind. The trading up associated with more, better and faster may yield some practical results but the net yield factored against the time it takes to produce the given result is thin and the net value of the dollar differentials involved are usually insufficient to make a dramatic difference in your life-style, especially when adjusted for inflation. As you run faster in this realm of more, better and faster, the treadmill also seems to be speeded up so that, at a point on the continuum, you are apt to have to run at full throttle to be running in place.

The magic of trading up operates on different principles. More, better and faster do not apply. The magic of trading up can transfigure an apple into a pineapple into a pine tree into a calendar of Christmases. It is transcendent. It is the quantum leap that gracefully and elegantly outdistances forever the world of time clocks and bosses and annual salary reviews. The principle that guides the magic of trading up is multiplication. The application of this kind of multiplication lies in discovering the essence of what you do best and find most congenial, distilling it and raising it to what we may call its highest paranormal numerator (the full spectrum apart from its lowest common denominator) in a way that produces a product or service that contains this distilled essence, and then transfiguring it so as to make it qualitatively different and immeasurably more valuable.

Let's examine the concept of the magic of trading up by breaking it down into its component parts and then putting the parts back together again. Most people are aware of the non-magical concept of trading up in terms such as those considered above, a convenient illustration of which is the buying of a better and/or newer automobile by using the old car as a downpayment. This process involves the use of "what one has" as a partial payment for "what one wants." This is done routinely and credit is usually the facilitating mechanism that permits a person to get "what he or she wants" at once without paying for it in full on delivery. Transactions of precisely this type have greatly expanded the United States economy and have acted as midwife in giving us the highest standard of living in the world. However, in the process, we have incurred an enormous burden of debts.

The magic of trading up involves the use of a magic-laden variation of this concept and applying it, not to spending money but to earning it. In the typical money-earning situation, a person who either does or does not have a job or other income-producing means, wants to produce or create additional earnings. He or she, in effect, is willing to trade skills or abilities or whatever, plus time, for money. If most people are more or less qualified for the job or other income-producing situation sought, they are, in effect, paying in full on or before delivery; if they are overqualified, they are over-paying, If they are underqualified, there is some probablility they will not get or keep the job or other income-producing situation, unless the underqualifications are slight. There is, therefore, no operative concept of "credit" or "deferred payment" that permits us to get "something we want" now; i.e., more money, without, in effect, paying for it in full. The most effective way to forge this connecting link to our success is to apply a multiplier effect to our efforts.

The earning and spending relationships are not reciprocal, as we have seen. We are able to use credit in the process of spending money but unable to do so in the process of earning money. The not too surprising result is that the usual mode of earnings advancement in job situations is a slow process involving limited pay rises at annual, or other infrequent, intervals. It is only when we change job titles that we may expect any substantial earnings increases. Such a change, however, ordinarily requires that we spend a certain amount of time in the previous job slot and learn new, transferable skills. Thus, delay is built into the one means we ordinarily have for meaningful increases in income, and inflation and rising expectations combine to keep this kind of gain substantially in check, putting us back close to the starting line again.

The first element of the magic of trading up involves the discovery of your long suit, what it is you do best and find most congenial. In making this discovery, approach the problem with as few preconceptions about what is and is not possible as you can. Don't allow your thinking to be bound by conventions. If you can look at a book of matches not only as a convenient means of lighting smoking materials, or igniting other combustibles but as a game element, a door check, a table leveler, an advertising medium, a scrap of writing paper, etcetera, you're on the right track. Use your imagination; look for the butterfly in the caterpillar. Don't be locked in or too literal.

Not too many years ago, the management of one of the country's industrial giants, International Business Machines, began to rethink their corporate concept by looking at the problem from a fresh point of view. They discovered that they really were not in the business of manufacturing and selling and/or leasing business machinery but that their real business was moving and processing information. Following that key insight, the company's fortunes began to soar.

Say, for example, you are a high school teacher of physical education. You have a relatively high degree of job security but the pay is not especially attractive and the chances for meaningful advancement in the system are not significant. The essence of what you do best and what you like to do is to distribute information in a personal, face-to-face way and let's further assume that your interests are fairly limited to physical education.

Having distilled this essence, the magic of trading up calls for raising it to its highest paranormal numerator. In other words, look at this essence, or nucleus, and transform it into a real trading up, one that facilitates a multi-plier effect. It is this multiplication of your efforts that will make a difference in your life. The transformation in-volved in this kind of meaningful, life-changing trading-up does not involve getting the same job in a better location, preparing for the hurdles of becoming chairper-son of the department or otherwise rising in the hierarchy of the school system, doing a similar job at the college level, or adding an extracurricular job of coaching one of the school's teams. All of these possibilities provide only incremental, non-magical changes. In terms of their effect on your life-style as a high school teacher of physical ed-ucation, they won't make a big difference.

You may, however, have noticed that driver education is a growing phenomenon and, in view of the highway accident rates, a valuable service. You might consider working out an arrangement that involved contracting to supply this service in a particular area and the hiring of other competent instructors as assistants. As there would be a differential between what you paid your assistants and the values they brought to your enterprise, the more assistants working profitably for you, the greater the mul-tiplier effect.

You may have the ability to write or commission the writing of a book that sets forth your own system of driver education. Such a book might be sold to other driver education classes as well as through the regular book distribution channels. The same essence, namely the distribution of information about applications of physical education, is simply packaged differently. This would combine well with your driver education school and would help extend this activity into other areas of the city, continually cloning it with the help of media and in-per-son publicity appearances.

The same thought process might yield a chain of exer-cise parlors in which aerobic exercises were done to musical accompaniment, a camp specializing in one or more sports, a weight-control business, an executive fitness program, a newsletter, or some other compatible enterprise, depending upon the nuances of the particular person's combination of interests, abilities, skills, how much risk he or she cared to take and to what extent it were possible to try out the new concept without abandoning the relative safety of the old career. There are at least a dozen other businesses this person could organize and an equal number of career changes (not simply different jobs as a physical education teacher) this person could create by applying the magic of trading up.

Had this teacher taught, say, geography, instead of physical education, he or she might have segued into the travel business, perhaps specializing in teacher travel, augmenting the gross receipts by offering a computerized apartment and automobile exchange program for traveling teachers all over the world, and eventuating in a global travel franchise. This teacher, as well as the physical education teacher, could have applied the magic of trading up without immediately resigning from his/her teaching job. Each could have begun in after-school hours and during summer vacations. Each could have arranged to be paid while learning, utilizing the concept of on-the-job training. Each could have gained valuable experience and knowledge and some new skills at somebody else's expense and have gotten paid for these efforts, and each could have developed his or her own special expertise that would have facilitated the next transition.

All skills, including those of the unemployed and the never-before-employed, are transferable into income-producing situations. The magic of trading up is not concerned with merely translating such packages of skills and time into the earning of money (although this process may be extremely worthwhile in individual cases), but with *transforming* them into ever so much more valuable potentials. Such translations are only additive; they are not de-signed to make you rich. The magic of trading up involves exponential advances, the explosiveness of multiplication. It is concerned not with providing you with a better job, but with a better life.

It isn't always necessary, or even desirable, in trading up to your own business, to incur large fixed expenses and other major responsibilities. With some thought and inge-nuity, you may be able to tie your product or service into an existing means of distribution. Once you allow your thinking to roam freely in the largely frictionless atmo-sphere of "highest paranormal numerator" conceptualiz-ing, breakthroughs become such a regular occurrence, you expect them and even anticipate them.

Maybe your product or service is something that could be distributed by corner newsstands in cities during rush hours, when lots of people are going to work and returning to their homes. Maybe it has something to do with an item that goes with breakfast or dinner or after breakfast and pre-dinner. Maybe the telephone lines or the mails are the best means of distribution for you, or a new kind of vend-ing machine. Maybe you could create some concentrated interest at no cost with a chain letter; not the kind that violates the law by offering an illegal pyramid scheme, but one that is sent by satisfied customers, the first among them being people known to you who are actually satisfied with your product or service and personally recommend-ing it to their friends, and so on, creating a new kind of launching for your venture. If the concept you create lends itself to the utilization of an existing pattern of distribution or to other existing resources (like, for example, adding your item or items to an existing sales force's line), you may then begin to direct your thinking to new ways of mining this available resource.

In each of the above examples, the effect is to multiply your efforts so that you receive a multiplied benefit. If you do a day's work for a day's pay, you are not receiving any multiplier effect for your efforts. As a general rule, multiplication of your efforts comes about by doing something that is essentially reproducible without your further efforts, in which you have ownership or other proprietary or contractual interest, or by employing others to add more value to your enterprise than the value of their recompense.

Examples of the former type of multiplication are a record album, a videotaped television series, and a theatrical motion picture. The record, the series and the movie are all reproducible. The combination of talent and other resources it took to create such products need be combined only once. If the product is successful, it can be duplicated and sold (or licensed) repeatedly and its useful life, via copyrights, is long.

The same general multiplier effect applies to ordinary mass-produced items. Products of your mind may also lend themselves to this approach. By packaging your efforts into a reproducible product or service, and/or organizing a business that utilizes the work product of others in a way that compensates them less than the increments they add to the value of your organization, you may be able to multiply your efforts and vastly increase the benefits you derive from these efforts.

A book, for example, need only be conceived and created once. It may thereafter be reproduced independently, without any further effort of its author, who ordinarily owns its copyright. It may ultimately yield income to its author not only in the print medium (hard and softcover editions, book clubs, foreign rights, syndication in newspapers, serialization in magazines, excerpts, etcetera), but it may be reproduced in one form or another on audiotapes, it may spin off into one or more movies, it may spawn one or more television series, and it may lead to a syndicated column or a series of similar books, the process repeating itself. It may even lead to the merchandizing of products.

Almost anything you discover to be your long suit may provide an opportunity for this kind of multiplication or for multiplying the effect of what you do through the input of others. To cite a mundane example of the latter approach, consider the occupation of "baby-sitter." I've deliberately chosen an occupation that is rather low-paid. Looked at from the point of view of a job, it doesn't provide much income. However, viewed as a business opportunity, it might.

There are, for example, hotels in every major city in this country that cater to conventions and other business meetings. These meetings are usually scheduled by major corporations or industry groups and they involve the transportation of hundreds, sometimes thousands, of people. They usually last from a few days to a week or so. Often, young children are taken along, sometimes as part of a family vacation to be combined with the business trip. These young children spend a great deal of time in the company of baby-sitters, the hotel often providing special suites of rooms in which a dozen or more children are looked after by three or four baby-sitters.

Somebody has to supply the baby-sitters. A subsidiary reward to the baby-sitters is that they are each responsible for a number of children, each of whom costs the guest the going hourly rate. This permits the individual or company supplying the labor to take a percentage of each hourly payment and still amply reward the baby-sitters in relation to the ordinary rates paid to baby-sitters, making it relatively easy to attract more competent people.

Lest this example seem fanciful, let me report a remarkable story I heard several years ago. During the nineteenth century, a poor woman, faced with the problem of supporting herself and her young son, found herself reduced to her last bit of flour. Undaunted, she made a batch of biscuits and took them to the railroad laborers, who bought every biscuit she'd made. With these proceeds, she bought more flour and repeated the process. This was the beginning of what became Nabisco, the National Biscuit Company, a company that has been listed on the New York Stock Exchange and has been paying dividends every year since 1899.

This courageous woman's story is not an isolated example of individual success. Thousands of people each year are becoming the principal players in their own success stories. Although it is considerably easier for an individual to become a millionaire in this century than it was in the last, many have needlessly given up the dream of transforming their lives by their own efforts.

The real misfortune of our system is not low productivity, garden variety incompetence and indifference, chronic unemployment or the unemployability of millions. These are taking a heavy toll but they are by-products, not causes. The more basic malady involves the widespread notion that no matter what you do, you can't hack your way through the jungle of "the way things are" to daylight. The hopelessness this kind of thinking fosters creates a heavy chain of unhappy consequences. However, once a person reaches the exhilarating realization that the results of his or her actions may make an important difference in his or her life, a link in that chain is smashed. The magic of trading up is simply a facilitating mechanism for creating this realization and making this liberating process more available.

IX

The Entrepreneurial Factor

There is a physical law to the effect that the accumulation of matter is facilitated in the presence of other matter and/or energy. In the precipitation of snow, for example, the condensation required to create snowflakes occurs about dust particles. The precipitation of wealth is governed by a similar law. Vacuums, by definition, are rather unproductive. As energy and matter coalesce under conducive conditions, they create dramatic physical changes. These same raw materials are the elemental requirements for the creation of wealth.

A formal business organization provides a facilitating structure or channel in which the multiplier effect of your efforts, referred to in a previous chapter, may be directed. The usual considerations that determine the choice of business organization to be created in a given instance involve questions related to the protection of business and personal assets, provisions for the growth of the business, continuity and transfer of ownership, tax consequences, the provisions of various benefit packages, and other matters affecting when, how, and how much you and others you designate will derive of the productivity of the business. A little planning with competent professional advisers should yield a form tailored to your specific needs and desires and one that can be fine-tuned easily as conditions and circumstances change. You will then be in the happy frame of mind of knowing that the success of your enterprise will yield the maximum desired net benefits that are legally possible.

As was set forth in detail in the previous chapter, a day's pay for a day's work is essentially a break-even operation. The realization of substantial wealth requires a means by which you can multiply the effects of your efforts so that you receive what would otherwise be the equivalent of several days' income from a single day's output. This "multiplier effect" is ordinarily achieved by producing products or services that lend themselves to reproduction without further proportionate effort on your part, or to the organizing of the work product of others so that the difference between their productivity and their remuneration results in multipliable profits for you.

Good ideas and the best intentions are relevant but without execution they remain only unproductive potentials. The "execution" specialists are the entrepreneurs, the people with enough vision and energy and knowhow to not only see the overview but to be able to interconnect all of the separate parts into a productively functioning whole. It is the entrepreneur who develops a business, takes the risks and, if successful, reaps the big rewards.

It should be clearly stated that, despite the extremely high financial rewards that go to the successful entrepreneur in our society, and all of the benefits to others in the community entrepreneurial activity may produce, it may be an inappropriate occupation for a given individual. You may, for example, find the demands on your time put too great a strain on your family life or on your health. You may discover conflicting drives and needs that override your acquisition of wealth via the entrepreneurial route. Your own personal motivation may be inadequate or you may be haunted by the fear of failure and/or its consequences. You may be in a position in which valuable career benefits would be lost or greatly reduced if you left your present employment. You may be on the threshold of an important promotion. All of these factors would tend to increase your doubts about becoming an entrepreneur. You may not have much opportunity to proceed at present or you may feel slightly overwhelmed about confronting all of the pieces and skills required to launch a successful business of your own. There may be a host of economic and other conditions that make it difficult or unwise for you to make this commitment.

If you decide not to become an entrepreneur, you may still be able to benefit by applying some entrepreneurial skills to the management of other projects. At any rate, if you read the material presented in this chapter carefully, you may get a new insight into successful and unsuccessful entrepreneurial behavior and thought patterns and thus put yourself in a better position to help others follow this path to riches. In addition, and this may be an important consideration, there are many opportunities to make a direct, private investment in entrepreneurial ventures. An understanding of the factors that make for success in such ventures will aid you in making these decisions.

David C. McClelland and David G. Winter (with Sara K. Winter and Elliott R. Danzig, Manohar S. Nadikarni, Aziz Pabaney and Udai Pareek) have written a highly original and valuable book, *Motivating Economic Achievement* (The Free Press, New York; Collier-Macmillan Limited, London 1969), in which they set forth methods they used in India, Oklahoma, and in Washington, D.C., to field-test the theory that economic growth processes could be speeded up in an individual enterprise, a community, and a society, through the nurturing and development of a single characteristic they call "n Ach," the need for achievement.

The authors make out a strong case that (1) economic development is tied to entrepreneurial activity, which, in turn, is motivated by the need for achievement, a kind of quest for improvement, and that (2) the need for achievement (n Ach) can be taught. In moving toward higher levels of n Ach, both thought patterns and patterns of action are important. As an indicator of such thought patterns, what is of primary importance is the frequency of an individual's spontaneous thoughts about achieving or improving something or of overcoming obstacles.

The thinking involves a focus on doing something that will result in improving, increasing or expanding an achievement, as distinguished from thinking or fantasying about the rewards to be derived after something is done and/or the mere expression of interest in improvement or achievement. Even the thinking about the completion of a task on schedule does not qualify as "n Ach" thinking; what is required is thinking about doing it *better*. The achievement involves not merely in getting the job done but in detting it done faster or better.

The action patterns of achievers have been analyzed. McClelland and Winter state that "years of research show that people with high n Achievement tend to act in certain characteristic ways." In devising a course of training intended to enhance n Achievement, McClelland and Winter concentrated on the "four characteristic modes of acting" of people with high n Achievement.

First, these people "tend to set moderate goals for themselves and to work harder when the chances of succeeding are only moderately great." The reason postulated for this behavior is that it represents an attempt to maximize their feelings of satisfaction in reaching goals. If the goal is too easy, there would be little satisfaction in achieving it. If the goal is too difficult, it may be completely out of reach and therefore yield no satisfaction at all.

McClelland and Winter illustrate this characteristic with

a training tool based on the game of ring toss. Each trainee is given three quoits and shown a peg at a distance. The object of the exercise is to throw the quoits over the peg from any distance the trainee chooses. The results were interesting. Some stood so close to the peg they were virtually placing the quoit about the peg. Others stood so far away they practically assured their lack of success. A few seemed to choose distances from the peg at which their success was likely (but not assured) and adjusted the distances to the results obtained. This group's behavior is typical of people with high n Achievement.

The second characteristic McClelland and Winter found among those high in n Achievement is that they "prefer work situations in which they can take personal responsibility for the performance necessary to achieve the goal." They have confidence in their own abilities and consider themselves better able to reach their goals than their competitors. They don't like to gamble on situations over which they have no control, and for similar reasons, they don't like committee decisions. Both gambling and group decisions deprive them of the satisfaction of their need for personal responsibility in determining results.

The third characteristic of people with high n Achievement is their interest in knowing how they're doing. They like to see the direct relationship of their efforts in specific, measurable results. They tend to gravitate toward those situations, like businesses, that satisfy this need.

Fourth, McClelland and Winter found that those high in n Achievement show a greater "initiative in researching the environment." They try new approaches; they travel more; they seek out alternative means of accomplishing their objectives. They are not easily defeated. They are more active, they take greater initiative in beginning projects and businesses of their own and they appear to be more alert to new entrepreneurial opportunities.

Those who may wish to participate in the high rewards

accorded to successful entrepreneurs but who score low in n Achievement can develop entrepreneurial skills and improve their chances for success. Many of the people in this group are immobilized by the fear of failure. The experimental data confirm that the fear leads those suffering from it to avoid moderately difficult tasks (precisely the kind those high in n Achievement seek) in favor of either very easy tasks or extremely difficult tasks, or both, those avoided by people with high n Achievement. The very easy tasks virtually assure success, while the extremely difficult ones attach no blame or humiliation if they are not accomplished.

The action mode of those high in n Achievement is to set moderate goals and to work harder to reach them when the chances of success are only moderately great. Significantly, if a person low in n Achievement fails at an easy task, he or she will tend to stop trying to accomplish it, whereas if he or she fails at a difficult task, the tendency will be to keep trying to get it done. This pattern is obviously not designed to yield much in the way of results. The explanation for this behavior is that when the task thought to be easy has been shown by failure at it not to have been a sure thing, the fear of failure takes over and eliminates it as something to attempt to accomplish. The hard task has also been failed at but, in view of its level of difficulty, the failure to accomplish it is not taken personally. Further attempts are therefore not discouraged and if any success is achieved, it may be deemed a big victory. The ego protection sought practically assures little or no results.

An awareness of the thought and action patterns and the principles that guide successful entrepreneurs is of great practical value, convertible into wealth. First, if your own bent is entrepreneurial, the factors that make for entrepreneurial success can be marshaled to your banner. These skills can be learned and improved. A less than excellent entrepreneurial profile and background need not ensure a poor finish. Cracks and gaps can be buttressed and bridged. Even if your early childhood models were not ideal and your career record of success has not been spectacular, n Achievement, which corresponds with entrepreneurial ability, is an attainable goal. Like learning a language, the skills can be mastered. In addition, an understanding of the thought and action patterns involved will help you select personnel with whom to ally your own efforts.

Interestingly, according to McClelland and Winter, the particularities that make for entrepreneurial success are peculiar to entrepreneurial success. They do not correspond with the factors that would produce a good scientist or lawyer or general or even with top management of large corporations. Messrs. Bandler and Grinder, who were mentioned in a previous chapter in connection with neurolinguistic programming (NLP), are of the opinion that by systematically analyzing the behavior and thought patterns of exceptional and extraordinarily successful people, using NLP, they can make such excellence available to others.

McClelland and Winter seem to be saying much the same with respect to entrepreneurial expertise: "The scientific implication of the research findings is inescapable. If they want to do a better entrepreneurial job, then the scientific evidence shows that the means to that end is to learn to think, talk and act like a person with high n Achievement." Thus, there is much hope for those not privileged to have spent years growing up watching the entrepreneurial efforts of one or both parents ripen into productivity and success or to be apprenticed to an accomplished entrepreneurial master and thus given the entire broad sweep of running a business and not some narrow specialty.

Whether or not you intend to become a successful entrepreneur, there is a good reason to be able to identify the thought and action patterns that make for entrepreneurial success, beyond those already considered. Opportunities for direct, private investments in businesses are plentiful. Although the majority of new business ventures fail within two years, among those that survive and prosper, there are chances for enormous profits.

A few years ago, I invested some money in a new venture, a start-up situation founded by a friend of mine. It may be useful to run through a kind of checklist of the points that led to this investment decision. The most important consideration in this sort of situation is usually management. Who is the person in charge? In this case, the entrepreneur is a moderate risk-taker by nature. His personal stock portfolio contains only blue chips; not a single "cat" or "dog" in the lot. He likes to assume personal responsibility for achieving goals, is confident of his own abilities and considers himself better able to reach the goals he sets than his competitors to reach theirs. This, the second of McClelland and Winter's four characteristics of people with high n Achievement, is typical of pilots and this man is a licensed pilot with an instrument rating. He is also attentive to feedback and shows a great deal of initiative in "researching the environment," the third and fourth of McClelland and Winter's n Achievement action syndrome.

In addition, this man had been president of a corporation producing a similar product line to the one he intended to produce, located in the same geographical area, and his prospective customers included many of the same companies with whom he'd been doing business successfully for years. The fact that he had already been able to satisfy customers in the real world with actual products is extremely important. The company he'd operated also had a highly profitable track record and it was several times the size of the company he proposed to found.

He was extremely well trained, intelligent, capable and experienced in all phases of the proposed business and a man of exceptional personal integrity and honesty who commanded the respect of those with whom he'd done business. He also had a sound business plan good enough to prompt a bank to make a middle-six-figure loan offer and he was familiar with and experienced in every aspect of the business he proposed to operate, not merely a specialist in a narrow aspect of it.

Two other factors made this man a good bet to run his company successfully. First, his need for power, for manipulating and controlling others, is not especially high, and is clearly subordinate to his need for achievement. High power needs and the confrontations they breed work against productivity and profitability. In addition, his need for affiliation, that is, to be well thought of, to be well liked, is also subordinate to his need for achievement, by a wide margin. The need to be "Mr. Nice Guy" may not only cloud business judgments, but personnel tend to underperform for those high in this need and profit margins usually suffer accordingly.

These judgments are, of course, subjective and are presented here not as indications of how people should or should not behave. They are meant to describe a rather specific cluster of attitudinal and action patterns that, when present in strength, make for entrepreneurial success in our society as it is presently organized. At this writing, my friend's company has a net worth of a million and a half dollars. My pro rata share of the after-tax earnings in 1979 exceeded my entire investment. Early in 1980, the company acquired a highly profitable and compatible company, its first expansion by merger. From nonexistence, its gross sales have grown to an estimated 30 million for 1980.

My objective in investing in this company was a return of twenty times my money in five to ten years. During the next three to five years, it would be reasonable to expect the company to be sold for between five and ten million dollars. In the process of becoming a multimillionaire, my friend will have created valuable products, scores of jobs, profits for his investors and the banks with which the company deals, and dozens of other substantial benefits to the community and the society.

This process, the one by which my friend has become a successful entrepreneur and, in turn, a millionaire, is instructive but it doesn't involve magic. For a good chef to turn all of the necessary ingredients and equipment into a great meal is, perhaps, praiseworthy, but it requires no magic. To create a great meal despite a number of missing ingredients, by concocting equivalences out of what is available, or the whipping up of the necessary ingredients into a great meal by a complete novice, however, may require a bit of legerdemain.

Similarly, there is a kind of magic in creating for yourself, in high concentrations, those qualities you have discovered are deficient for the achievement of specific goals, and then reaching or surpassing these goals. In this case, this would involve converting a configuration of thought and action patterns low in n Achievement into a high n Achievement syndrome, followed by significant entrepreneurial success. A lower order of magic might involve increasing your own n Achievement and combining your entrepreneurial efforts with those of others into a successfully functioning business organization.

Entrepreneurial activity is the most widely traveled route to big money. Thousands of family fortunes have been created in this way and the process continues. I cited the example of my friend's business, one that he had brought from scratch, from non-existence, to within hailing distance of annual after-tax earnings of upwards of a million dollars within a relatively short time and from a small start-up base. He is a capable man but he is neither superhuman nor unique. Sufficiently motivated and trained, hundreds, if not thousands, of readers of this book can produce this level of personal wealth via entrepreneurialship.

Even if you have no desire to become a captain of industry, you may care to participate in some of the many benefits available through the mechanism of your own closely held corporation. Assuming that most, if not all, of the corporate income can be expensed out (including your salary), so that your efforts are not burdened by double taxation (both corporate and personal income taxes), you may, through corporate pension and profit-sharing plans, shelter up to 25 percent of the income the corporation pays you from all taxes, as well as all increments on these sums, which may be invested at your direction, until the funds are paid out to you after retirement. Deferred compensation may be placed into a program guaranteed by an insurance company, so that gains on (in effect) tax-free dollars are compounded until your retirement. You may even wish to invest some of these funds in a couple of carefully selected entrepreneurial ventures to be operated by others. In addition to salaries and bonuses, expense accounts, medical and life insurance, and a dozen other perks available through the corporation, there is, for many successful entrepreneurs, the great satisfaction of doing it "their way" and making it work to their personal benefit as well as to that of the people it affects.

X

Where the Money Trees Grow

Trees are hardy organisms that can survive adverse, even harsh, growing conditions. In order to thrive, however, each genus requires its own optimum environment. By any measurement, the difference between the stunted development of a tree continually subjected to poor conditions, and the majestic height, luxuriant foliage and successions of crops of luscious fruits or delicious nuts of another tree grown from a seed of the identical source, but raised under ideal conditions, is remarkable. So it is also with money trees. Not every nursery is ideally suited to the nurturing of each variety, and individual specimens will no doubt fare better the sooner they are transplanted to a more favorable environment.

Money trees represent a special cornucopia of riches and good fortune almost as rarely encountered as unicorns and seemingly only by others. They are mistakenly assumed to be in such short supply for two reasons. First, most of those who seek them look only where it is convenient to do so, not where they grow. Second, only a few people know how to recognize a money tree, even at short range.

Nevertheless, these big bonanza trees do exist and they can be yours if you are willing to follow reliable guidance.

Before proceeding with a description of what to look for and where and how to look, some general properties of money trees should be grasped, for a clear understanding of what they are must precede the search for yours if the latter is to prove fruitful. Although there exists, as generally acknowledged, an ecological web that interconnects all living organisms, the relationship between you and your money tree is much more intimate, immediate, direct and personal. Like many other varieties of valuable stock, money trees are highly perishable and depend upon faithful personal care. In fact, without your help and cooperation, your money tree cannot even push itself above ground level. Your money tree is so personal a reality, that, like the rabbit Harvey and his keeper, your money tree may be invisible to all but you, especially while it is still only a tiny sapling. So far from discouraging the engagement of your energies in its pursuit, this invisibility to others should be taken as evidence that you are at last on the right trail.

Whereas the ordinary tree falls soundlessly in the forest if it does so out of earshot, your money tree has no existence at all independent of its relationship with you. In short, your money tree represents opportunities that you create for yourself and from which you are the principal beneficiary. Should you decide to pass up these opportunities or ignore them or if you are unaware of them or ill-prepared or under-prepared to pursue them, the opportunities move on.

Preparation is thus the essential requirement in seeking, finding, and benefiting from, your money tree. Preparation requires some time and effort but these are prudent investments, for an initial small step in the right direction is obviously of much greater advantage than miles of aimless wandering in a maze at a later stage. In considering how best to travel the distance from where you are to where you want to be, consider how you would advise your twin. Most people are capable of a reasonable appraisal of their own strengths and weaknesses but they usually don't translate the appraisal into a plan of action. Even fewer people adhere to the plan long enough to execute it.

Even if you have strayed or drifted off course over the years, you have a vested interest in the status quo. It is familiar terrain; it represents a considerable investment of many precious resources, and there is a strong tendency to perpetuate bad investments. As with a stock you may be holding at a paper loss for years, you don't want to formalize the admission that you made a mistake by selling the stock and taking the loss. By viewing the problem of your becoming rich from the vantage point of your "twin," the emotional charge ordinarily put on the status quo is attenuated and you will tend to be more objective.

The purpose of this phase of preparation is to suggest the most compatible growing conditions you and your money tree share, as an aid to selecting for yourself an initial transplantation site. Many people quickly settle for convenience. They attend the nearest school instead of the best one available to them because it is convenient. They take the first job offered instead of the best one they can get. Choices, alternatives, are almost always at hand, even if not always immediately recognized. By limiting yourself to only what is obviously available, you needlessly restrict your angle of elevation. The acceptance of convenience is not designed to produce optimum results and it rarely does so. The predictable result is underachievement, wasted potentials, and often, a life of unfulfillment and vague dissatisfactions.

The charting of a new course presents a genuine opportunity to rescue yourself from past error and future disappointment. If you are one of those fortunate people who "always" wanted to be involved in a specific career, you had an easy goal toward which to direct yourself. In your own way, you began to attune your antennae to greater sensitivity to this passionate interest. In time, you became more knowledgeable in your field of special interest. Others noticed this self-direction and may have helped and encouraged you. If, along the way, you did not abandon this dream, you are, or were, probably part of this occupational group, or within striking distance of it, even if not precisely in the aspect of it that originally seized your interest. The transitional and transformational moves required to claim your money tree will be relatively easy for you.

If you drifted away from this early passion or never felt strongly attracted to a specific career, you are one of millions of people who let the ball play them instead of vice versa. The trail to your money tree may have become overgrown; it may even be "cold," but it nevertheless exists. In a quiet moment, with the guidance and counsel of your compassionate "twin," you can begin to locate it.

In the process of discovering the route to your money tree, ignore the "how" until you have determined the "what." The catalysts and the transitions and other modes of travel will be considered at a later stage. Before you decide the best way to get there, you must determine where you want to go.

As an aid to discovering your destination, look for what was referred to in a previous chapter as the highest paranormal numerator of the essence of what you do best (or would like most to do) and what you do, or would, find most congenial. If what you do best happens not to be the same kind of work as that which you consider most congenial as a long-term career goal, the latter should be accorded greater weight. In the enchanted forest where your money tree grows, passion is much more important than competence or experience and, if genuine, will yield both more intense, and longer-term, satisfactions.

You must decide what you want to do with a large block of career time. It should be something that suits you, that feels right to you. It is your own personal choice. If your father-in-law wants you to be an admiralty lawyer and you feel strongly about raising dogs, you should have the right to respect these feelings and to act them out. Both you and your father-in-law, presumably, want you to be happy and successful. You and he are entitled to differ respectfully about how you should go about it. There is no compelling reason to suppose you will both come to the same conclusion at the same time.

Your decision may require a great deal of introspection. Maybe your long-term career goal is something you thought about as a child but haven't considered recently. Perhaps it has to do with something you'd like to change or improve. Don't rush the process. You will not have reached a forward-going decision until you and your "twin" are satisfied.

If you are comfortable with your choice of a field of interest, activity or industry, it is time to generalize this choice as a prelude to raising it to its highest paranormal numerator. The generalization will later yield a dozen entry points for making the first transitional move en route to your objective. For example, the generalization "communication" includes thousands of occupations that span the broadcasting industry, the print medium, entertainment, the arts, public relations and a fairly long list of lesser inclusive generalizations, each of which includes scores of specific occupations as different from one another as the person who "warms up" the audience prior to the taping of a television game show and a skywriter. To take another generalization, if, for example, you decided you were interested in "statistical research," it is obvious this interest has applications in almost every business, profession, branch of government, and so on.

The next step in the decision-making process is to have

a conversation with your "twin" about what you would like your occupation to be in five to ten years. Give yourself the benefit of the doubt but stay comfortably within the real world. Are you currently part of a large or small company? Are you in your own business? Are you in one of the professions? Are you a government worker?

Consider your present occupation, if you have one. Unless it is a temporary job, examine how well you have managed your career. Have you packaged and orchestrated the right combination of elements for yourself, and placed yourself in the right place at the right time for maximum advancement? If you work for a company, for example, and your department isn't one that makes a crucial difference in the fortunes of the company, you probably aren't being paid on the same scale as those whose efforts are considered pivotal to the company's success. Are you one of the stars of your workplace or only a supporting player? If the organization that employs you has twenty branch offices and yours is seventeenth in productivity, don't expect personal miracles no matter how good you are. The same applies if your company is ranked ninety-seventh in its industry. A star athlete doesn't get superstar contract offers from a D League team. Your money tree is much more likely to be found where the money action is and your willingness to relocate, if necessary, will facilitate this quest.

It is easy to resist relocation. You may miss Charlie and Lila next door, as well as Billie's school, so carefully selected. These losses, and others, are undeniable but there are empathetic neighbors and good schools where your money tree grows and Charlie and Lila may visit, and you and Billie may write and telephone your relatives and friends.

In these pages, economic and financial considerations are admittedly emphasized. The subject of the book is, after all, wealth. This emphasis, however, does not imply that non-money considerations are irrelevant. It is some-times convenient to allow fear of the unknown, inertia, lack of purpose and poor planning to masquerade as one or another non-money consideration. One or more of these reasons becomes the peg on which to rationalize inaction, the perpetuation of the status quo. Then, too, other peo-ple's imputed interests are accorded great weight (often without any discussion with the person involved) and used to bolster the hesitancy to risk seeking a better life. We, of course, would be willing to give it our best shot, but we're willing to make the "sacrifice" (and stay where we are) "for the kids" or "for our parents" or other loved ones, or in the name of somebody else.

How anybody decides the question of relocation is a private matter in each case. There are risks and inconve-niences but I would respectfully suggest that a self-charted course can be more exhilarating and more rewarding than drifting with the currents and that movement and growth are life-enhancing and inherently superior to stagnation. This approach is essentially a variation on a basic law of success to the effect that if what you're doing doesn't work, do something else. A change of address is not absolutely necessary in every case. While money trees are not found in equal numbers throughout the world, they do grow in some number, however small, almost everywhere. Those who do not wish to seek them where they grow in stands should be willing to cultivate intensively those they can find nearer at hand. The upside to relocation is that the value of your career, even if you decide not to become an entrepreneur, may be increased by two or three hundred thousand dollars or more, not including the profit on your house, if you decide to buy one, and your life-style along the way is likely to be significantly more satisfying.

Whether you are self-employed or not, *where* you work is as important as *what* you do in terms of the reasonably probable financial returns. As suggested earlier, most people who are unaware of money trees accept the first job offer they receive. It is usually located in the city or town in which they've been living. Not surprisingly, this haphazard beginning does not augur a brilliant or a fulfilling career. Perhaps this explains at least some of the continual chafing of job dissatisfaction and low productivity. The total costs of this kind of "convenience" are enormous. Fortunately, you can do something to change this pattern of self-limitation. Once you have determined what you want to do with your career, where you want to be a few years hence, and have realized the difference getting there will make to your life and those close to you between your achieving a level of success in the middle range of your potential and the top range you can produce, why not ignore the fear of failure and give it your best shot?

Even if you think you're not ready to make the move, begin to "research the environment." Where is the real action in your company or industry, both conceptually and geographically? If you are not presently engaged in the same field in which your long-term career goal lies, would it help you to segue into the "action" area of your company before leaping the chasm into your chosen field or is the reverse the superior option for you to consider now? At this stage in your planning, the overall strategy is too vague and fragile to discuss with anybody but your "twin." You will be better able to discuss your plan with those closest to you after you have determined both your long-term career goal and the first transitional objective en route, particularly if your proposed course will have to be defended vigorously.

The facts are rather easily developed. A high-fashion clothing boutique might reasonably be expected to gross considerably more in Beverly Hills or Houston than in Cadiz, Ohio, or Linden, New Jersey. Similarly, there is a best "where" to be matched with the specific "what" you plan to do. In two or three trips to a good public library, you may, with a little help from the librarians, rather easily come away with a list of the dozen or so most likely cities in which to get on with your career, arranged in order of their statistical desirability.

This list would take account of a number of factual conditions. For example, what is the job market like? What are the local trends in your chosen field? Is money flowing into the area and, if so, at what rate? What do the population trends indicate? What about housing, property values, schools, industry, cultural and recreational facilities, the social life of the community, the climate, transportation? You will be able to get answers to scores of factual questions from a library chair. This may not be an adequate substitute for firsthand experience of the locations but it should be sufficient to enable you to eliminate a number of the candidates, shortening your list. Your personal preferences, and those of all of the people who will be going with you, may then be factored into the mix, out of which should emerge about three or four possible locations, arranged in a rough order of overall preference.

After you have made some decisions on the "what" and "where," it is time to consider the "how." At first glance, you may be inclined to consider the task unmanageable. This should be interpreted as a favorable indication. You are being serious. You have had the courage to make a significant, personal choice, something that means a great deal to you, instead of settling for an easy way out. You have avoided the trap of "convenience."

You may recall that two of the characteristics of people with high n Achievement considered in a previous chapter were the willingness to take moderate risks (not wild risks and not no risks at all) and the setting of moderate goals and working harder to reach them when their chances of success were only moderate. These two characteristics can be adapted and applied to the logistics involved in getting "there" from "here."

If you've ever been involved in following a set of driving directions from your house to that of a friend or relative, you will readily understand the process involved in the trip. The major objective of reaching their address was divided into a number of minor objectives along the route. You may have gotten lost en route and had to double back or cut across a road not included in the original plan. You may have had to travel a long distance before you reached the main highway, the one that would take you most of the way there, or maybe it was nearer at hand than you thought it would be. You may have had to ask for help along the way. You may have encountered adverse road and/or weather conditions not originally contemplated, or perhaps the car broke down. Nevertheless, you had confidence in the directions and in your ability to find your way, even without ever having made the trip before and without your being able to see the destination from your point of origin.

In managing the transitions, your ability to relate to people will be valuable. As you move forward, if you find you don't have any of the important elements you will need to propel you, look for ways to supply what's missing without interrupting your flow of income. The practice of "on-the-job-training" became widespread during World War II, during which millions of people who were inexperienced and untrained in scores of essential occupational skills were brought up to high levels of competence while being paid to learn in the workplace. You may utilize this concept, not only by "stretching" a bit in a transitional job, and then growing into it, but also by learning (formally or informally) in order to qualify for the next move. Many companies make certain educational benefits available to their employees if the courses are reasonably job-related. This relatedness is usually rather broadly interpreted. It is a good idea to avail yourself of this opportunity if you can. Not only will you benefit from the content of the courses but the company, having made this investment, has a stake in your advancement. In addition, you will have distinguished yourself from others who lack this training and you will have demonstrated your initiative in obtaining it while working. These factors will all work in your favor in facilitating job title changes within the company, as well as transfers to the "action" areas of the company. The expenses, of course, will be borne by your employer. If you are self-employed or a principal in a business, keep the initial mistakes you may make in a new area as small as possible. Try to find somebody who will pay you to make your next transitional move, or at least share the costs.

If you work for a large company, look at it as a supermarket of opportunities. Find out the locations of all of the branch offices and the various job titles in the entire organization. Make up your own table of organization, so that you can see at a glance how all of the parts are interrelated and who reports to whom and who is in charge of what. You should do the same with the major competitors of your company, so that you may become aware of additional opportunities your company does not offer. It may well be that a minor promotion or even a lateral move to a competitor will make available an opportunity in the competing company your company doesn't offer, and put you miles closer to your money tree.

As you move toward your objectives, try to distinguish yourself and your products or services without overselling yourself. Keep up your energy level and your enthusiasm. Do more than you have to, more than your share, and do it as well as you can. Good value given with good will will earn you recognition and put the wax on your skis. Keep at it. Don't make the common mistake of giving up if your early efforts are not immediately overtaken by success. There is a definite relationship between your efforts and their results but the flow of benefits to you often requires some pump priming. Go with the momentum of your career that you create but try to foresee where the transitions occur naturally. Only by treating your relationship with your career with respect will you truly understand it and be capable of taking it to new limits.

XI

People Rhythms

No individual is always the same. In fact, with all of the continuous atomic, biomolecular, psychological, physiological and other systemic activity going on in our minds and bodies, it is, perhaps, remarkable we are able to recognize one another, much less to interact harmoniously, joyfully, productively and profitably. Each of us is immersed in a sea of environmental variables. Light, temperature, barometric pressure, humidity, cosmic rays, lunar and solar phases, electromagnetism, color and sound, to cite only the most obvious, all register their changes on the human body and each creates effects. In addition, at the same time as you are subjected to a welter of outer influences, you carry about within a continuously shifting, complex labyrinth. The ebb and flow of your many physiological and psychological systems, your rising and falling blood pressure, body temperature, respiration, pulse rate, hemoglobin and blood sugar levels, and other variables, produce myriad changes in your emotions, health and well-being, physical and mental abilities, and even affect the length of your life.

You change from day to day and from day to night. You have your good days and bad days and even your good and bad hours of the day. Although each of us differs markedly from all others in the precise orchestration of all of the variables at any given point in time, your individual shifts and changes are not random, but occur in rather predictable, rhythmic cycles. If you were able to learn your own major cyclical patterns and the stimuli that affect you most, you would be able to "press" a little harder on your good days and ease off the throttle a bit on the bad days, for maximum results and benefits. In addition, if you were able to schedule your business and social intercourse with others on days when they were most receptive and in circumstances and settings that were most conducive to your objectives, you would gain a formidable and valuable advantage. How to accomplish these goals is the subject of this chapter.

The Foundation for the Study of Cycles in Pittsburgh told me the question of financial gain through "people rhythms" was "ahead of its time." Further research did not develop what I sought. Nevertheless, there may be sufficient straws in the wind from which much gold may be spun. I decided to examine the work on biorhythms and to push on from there.

Much has been written about biorhythms, the cyclical ups and downs that occur in living organisms with a high degree of regularity, or pattern. Researchers, widely separated both geographically and in time, have concluded that there are, in effect, biological time clocks would up and set within each of us at birth that govern our shifts and swings of mood, intellect and physical condition. Each of these three major life cycles, of emotions, mind and body, repeats its own regular movements throughout the course of a lifetime. Mort Gale, in *Biorhythm Compatibility*, postulates a fourth major cycle, which he calls "intuitional."

You have, no doubt, experienced days during which you were unaccountably cheerful, happy, optimistic; there was no specific event or outcome in your life that might explain this good mood. You were simply having one of your "up" days. You have also observed other people on their good and bad days. Those having a "bad" day are generally irritable and/or depressed for no apparent reason. According to biorhythm theory, one complete cycle of this "emotional" series of changes takes twenty-eight days.

In similar fashion, you have days on which your mind seems to be functioning at peak levels. You are quick, accurate, efficient; your mental processes are in overdrive. You rapidly grasp new ideas and concepts and your creative output is high. The reverse is also true. Some days, nothing clicks into place as it should. Your mind is simply unable to work properly. You're out of sync with your environment, not keen or sharp mentally. You make errors; you're inefficient and can't seem to get anything done. This cycle of intellectual capabilities is said to be thirty-three days in length.

The third major life cycle, the physical, takes twenty-three days, according to the proponents of biorhythm. On a good day, you feel strong and healthy. Your timing and coordination are sharp. You feel invigorated. During the opposite phase of this cycle, you simply don't feel well. You may or may not be physically ill or stricken, but you are aware that you are not up to par. You feel weak, tired, drained, like a rundown battery. You are stressed, your output is labored, almost any physical exertion is a strain.

Mort Gale contends there is a fourth major life cycle, the intuitional, which is thirty-eight days in length. This cycle represents, in Mr. Gale's view, variations in the ability to pick up information through "unconscious inner perceptions," such as occur in "hunches" or "intuitions."

Mr. Gale's book includes the most convenient and easily used tables and charts I know of, so that anybody interested may derive the relevant numbers for all four of the major life cycles in a minute or two, provided the birthdate of the subject is known. Each of the four numbers indicates at what point in each respective cycle a particular person happens to be on a given day, whether he or she is in an "active" or "passive" phase of each cycle, whether any phase is at a "critical" point, as well as the relationships among the four cycles. The numbers for future and past dates are as easily derived as those of a current date, and Mr. Gale provides what he calls the "Gale phase plot," which allows the relative relationships among the four cycles to be seen as they move over the course of about a fortnight. Most of these relationships are said to occur in a fairly neutral zone. However, there are high and low points in particular combinations that produce signals of unusual "internal weather conditions" and which require particular attention and special management.

Despite the supporting examples supplied by the proponents of biorhythms, I remain unconvinced that a) one's birthdate controls these cycles throughout one's life, and b) the cycles are as precisely and rigidly defined as postulated. Nevertheless, the underlying principles of the cyclical nature of many of the important aspects of life are both sound and useful. There are ups and downs in human psychology and physiology. Therefore, even if there is no scientific validity to biorhythm tables and charts as such, an awareness of cyclical phenomena is important. By learning to rely on your own observations of yourself and others, not only with respect to the so-called major life cycles, but in realms far beyond, that include personal preferences, daily routines and habit patterns, you can adjust your schedule (to the extent possible) so that the important events in your life occur on favorable days. You may also be enabled to manage your schedule so that your more delicate interactions with others dovetail with their individual preferences, routines and patterns in order that harmony and success are maximized.

In addition to scheduling advantages, by becoming sensitive to, and more observant of, these variables in yourself and others, you create opportunities to shift gears when the storm warnings become evident. You may shorten work sessions, confine the business of the meeting to pre-liminaries, and/or reschedule on "bad" days. When con-ditions appear favorable, you would tend to press. This would give you the overwhelming advantages of being in the right place at the right time with the right people

If, on the other hand, biorhythms produce such regular (although individual) patterns that they can be accurately catalogued and tabulated solely on the basis of a person's birthdate, the value of this tool (of people rhythms) is greatly enhanced. To the extent within your control, you would simply schedule your business life for maximum return on your own cyclical highs and for a lighter calen-dar, shorter work sessions and more rest, recuperation and recovery on critical days, with a general skew sensitive to your active and passive phases.

In relationships with others, you would become, in ef-fect, an "ace major league pitcher" with a complete "book" on everybody you faced, by virtue of your knowledge of their birthdate and a minute or two of simple calculations with biorhythm tables, available in a number of works on the subject. You would more easily close deals with others during or near the tops of their active phases, when they were optimistic, feeling good, expansive and receptive, nimbly avoiding their periods of passivity and irritability. If you were able to select days for these meetings when you and the other principal were especially compatible, you would reinforce and build a favorable personal rela-tionship. Others would begin to perceive you, perhaps un-consciously at first, as good company, a positive influence. This would give you the best of both worlds. That is, you would enjoy the amiable, pleasant side and avoid the moody, cantankerous, hostile aspects of an individual's personality.

In adversary relationships, you could, if you wished to, and to the extent possible, arrange matchups when you were at or near the top of your form and your opponent were "under the weather." Harmony and handshakes, with signatures to follow, for your deals, smashing victories and the overwhelming of your opponents in combat. A bit much to expect from biorhythms alone, perhaps, but there are many other aspects of people rhythms that may be used to your advantage.

Quite apart from the so-called major life cycles postulated by the proponents of biorhythms, each of us has a personal style linked to habit patterns and preferences, environmental cues and inner drives, the hourglass and the calendar. Although your general notions of the various personal terrains of those with whom you interact may be sufficient for a broad range of everyday activities, the magic of thinking rich requires more skillful, better observed, cartography. Individual differences always create opportunities for harmony or cacophony, amiability or irritability, triumphs or disasters, and, more to the point in this context, profit or loss. If you wish to maximize your profit-making opportunities, you must learn how to vary your pitch. This will require close attention to the observable data.

One of the clearest divisions among your associates is their characteristic circadian rhythm. Is a particular individual nocturnal or diurnal, an "owl" or a "lark"? Habit patterns, blood chemistry, hormonal balances and other psychological and physiological variables produce marked differences in mood and performance levels of both owls and larks during their respective waking hours. The fluctuations of both groups occur over essentially the same range and produce similar change ratios during their respective "normal" days. However, as larks tend to rise and retire earlier than owls, the two groups are usually out of sync with one another. Thus, it might be a matter of serious consequences whether one's surgeon or attorney were on one's case at a time of day he or she found congenial. In fact, I would not even want to schedule an appointment with my barber as his or her last cut of the day if he or she were a lark.

Thus, scheduling an early breakfast meeting with an owl will not produce maximum amiability or expansiveness in the creature and should be avoided unless it is part of your purpose to upset and disorient your unfortunate breakfast companion. Owls at early meetings are disruptive, or they tend to behave as turtles and keep their heads well within their respective carapaces, quietly seething, allowing them to protrude occasionally so that they may vent their displeasure. They may be willing to accept certain changes in a deal if they are minor, but they will tend to be out of sorts and should not be pressed. This is a bad time to propose a new venture or any major undertaking. Turtles don't take risks, especially from the head-in-carapace position.

Larks will tend to behave much the same late at night or in the wee hours of the morning. Any excessive stimuli (bright lights, high-decibel-level sounds, et cetera) will heighten the effects. A late-night or wee-hours-of-the-morning telephone call to the home of a lark will produce similar results except that, whereas the owl's disorientation will be about the same as the lark's, his or her resentment will tend to be muted. Owls are somewhat defensive about their late hours in our society. Larks, on the other hand, think of themselves as industrious, important, the vertebrae of the community, and they become self-righteous at disturbances in their routine. The disturbers are often judged to be bizarre.

If the mathematical precision attributed to the so-called major life cycles by the proponents of biorhythms should be found lacking, you may nevertheless be able to determine the phases of these cycles in yourself and among those of whom this knowledge would be most useful. The existence of rhythmic cycles in people and many of their significances and consequences are well documented and confirmed by a variety of experimental data. The menstrual cycle in women produces hormonal changes and a cyclical pattern of emotional responses, often including pre-menstrual tension. Men also experience a monthly cycle of hormonal changes.

An awareness of these cycles and a sensitivity to them will enable you to improve your position, even without your knowing exact dates. If, for example, you sense the appearance of this sort of monthly turbulence, don't put the deal on the table and don't press. Be as pleasant as you can and reasonably brief in your presentation. Don't move beyond the preliminaries and reschedule the important, decision-making meeting for two weeks later, if you can, when you are likely to encounter the top of the cycle. Note that any rescheduling, even if two weeks is too long to put the meeting off, will almost undoubtedly be an improvement for you.

Had the meeting gone well, or should the next one seem to coincide with a cyclical high, or at least avoid a low, the strategy would be to cluster your meetings with this person about this date. This approach would enable you to avoid the personal troughs and to seek the crests and active phases. Other things being reasonably equal, this scheduling technique should add a little bankable magic to your business meetings. If it is impractical to reschedule, shorten the lengths of the work sessions, keep the pressure low, and allow for more rest between work sessions if you or the key decision-maker with whom you're dealing are in a low phase.

Like all relationships, business relationships exist in a context. Factors exogenous of the business relationship may actually become determinative of business dealings. A sensitivity to these factors and a close appraisal of how they may affect the thoughts and feelings of the decision-makers in the particular dealing or business association will improve your timing and control.

For example, if an individual is heavily invested in the stock market, and is a worrier, you may not be able to influence the prices of equities, but you shouldn't have much difficulty scheduling your meetings to avoid such days as those on which the Federal Reserve Board meets or the consumer price index is made public or the whole-sale price index is announced or at times when data, to which the stock market is particularly sensitive, and which are scheduled at specific times that are known in advance, are made public, particularly in nervous markets or during bear market phases. On such days, plus or minus a day or two, if the news is unfavorable, the market may sell of sharply, chilling the atmosphere for your deal.

Your timing can also be improved by learning the daily routine and certain personal preferences of your opposite number. This is something like learning the customs of a country not your own and no less important. It is not an uncommon office practice, for example, to go through the mail and dictate some memos and letters early in the day, while most of the calls are held. Then, while a secretary types this work, your man or woman might attend some meetings, go to lunch, and take and return calls near the end of the business day.

If this is, in fact, the typical pattern of the crucial other, you would do best to accommodate this routine by getting your correspondence addressed to this person to arrive early in the day, perhaps by special messenger or telex or telegram with guaranteed delivery or some other delivery method that will distinguish it from most of the rest of the mail, so that it gets an attention preference. You would also place your calls late in the day, so they get right through or are returned with minimum delay. Calls that remain on the incoming call sheet for a few hours or more tend to become superseded by more current calls and repeating your call that remains unanswered tends to put you out of position, one down. Inertia, habit and routine thus work in your favor instead of the opposite and friction is thereby reduced. Whatever this person's business routine may be, he or she almost undoubtedly has typical times of the day when your mail, calls and meetings are most and least welcome.

You would also do well to learn the preferred setting a given individual with whom you are (or will be) doing business has for the conducting of business discussions. Does this person like to do business over a leisurely meal, and if so, which meal; or, is this person on a strict diet or have some other reason for wanting to avoid a business meal? If a meal is in order, in addition to food preferences, there are considerations of privacy, noise and lighting levels, ambience, convenience, amount of time and time of day to be factored into the choice of restaurant, club or private dining room before the best selection may be made. High-level meetings may also require the picking up and delivering of your guest to and from the meal, by limousine.

Some people prefer restaurant settings or other public places; others feel most comfortable and secure on their own turf and think it significant if they can get you to come to their office, especially during negotiating sessions. If this isn't overdone and if they don't take advantage of home base by wasting time and giving me considerably less than full attention, while they discourteously continue to conduct other business, I have no object to their being comfortable in their own lair. The point is that there are widely differing preferences, and it is a mistake to assume others share yours.

No two people are precisely synchronous or identical in the refinements of their sensory perceptions. If in doubt, move slowly. Ask; don't assume. In doing so, avoid "presumptuous" questions that lead the other person, or contain implicit conclusions ("Where do you want to eat lunch?" should not be asked until it is first established the other person wants to eat lunch), are omnibus, manifold, or rapid-fire, or are preemptive ("Would you like to eat at X or Y?" or, "French or Italian?" or, "I've reserved a table at Z.") Such questions and statements exhibit a lack of consideration for the other person. It is a mistake to underestimate either the ability of another person to detect this negative attitude or its adverse effects on you and your deal.

Avoid abrupt transitions into the business dealing, especially if the other person has had to travel to the meeting and/or you don't know him or her well or haven't seen the other recently. If the other person arrives at your office from the airport, it is not only rude, but counterproductive, to launch into the business purpose of the meeting. Everybody you'll be dealing with knows about jet lag and nobody will allow himself or herself to be disadvantaged by it. The other person will probably be offended by your insensitivity and discourtesy if you fail to make him or her welcome and comfortable before any serious discussions are commenced. If the other person or persons have crossed time zones to meet with you, they are likely to be somewhat disoriented and you will score points by demonstrating your sensitivity to their circumstance. If they are hungry, feed them, and suggest a place that will serve the kind of meal indicated by their inner clocks, not your watch.

Setting plays a part in creating a positive or negative predisposition to a transaction. Retail stores have discovered that they can increase sales by making the spending of money "fun." Music, lighting, set decoration and, increasingly, food and drink, sometimes accompanied by careful casting of the staff and some studied patter, combine to create a total environment designed to loosen your purse strings. Real estate agents in southern California have learned to used the same kind of mood massage that readies the prospective buyer to make a six- or seven-, sometimes eight-figure commitment for a residence and to spend more than was contemplated. The agent often drives a Rolls-Royce or a customized and specially appointed automobile of an even smaller production run and higher price, and tosses off the prices in casual abbreviations, quoting the prices of recent sales the office closed, at appropriately higher numbers than those of the properties you will be shown.

The purpose of developing your sense of people rhythms is to improve the odds in your favor for acquiring wealth. You can learn to become more aware of, and sensitive to, your own moods and feelings and those of the people with whom you interact, and modify your behavior accordingly. If you can thus eliminate the intrusion of a negative, or high-risk, factor, or add a compatibility factor, or, better still, substitute the latter for the former, you improve your chances for success. Over time, if you keep at it, these improved chances compound to produce dramatic, even magical, gains. The objective is to put you in the position, in effect, of winning if the coin comes up "heads," whereas if "tails" should appear, it doesn't count.

XII

How and When to Bet, Call, Raise and Fold . . . and When to Walk Away

Like people, events also have rhythms of their own which, if properly interpreted, are capable of yielding magical results. A highly developed sense of timing is crucial to successful speculation. In the *Book of Ecclesiastes*, it is well written, "To every thing there is a season, and a time to every purpose under the heaven." Sometimes ignored but equally true is the implication that not every season is propitious for every purpose. Conventional wisdom has it that what you lose on the turns you make up on the roundabouts. This is imprecise, casual thinking that more often leads to further losses than to evening up on the roundabouts. Wobbly wheels don't usually straighten themselves out. Trends tend to be self-perpetuating long enough to establish heavy financial losses if you are positioned the wrong way and allow yourself to be lulled by this sort of wishful thinking.

Even random or chance events will often produce a "streak," that is, a number of consecutive like occurrences, in apparent defiance of the laws of probabilities. Streaks are part of the rhythm of events and are, in reality, in accord with, not in opposition to, the laws of probabilities. For example, a coin specially designed and milled to produce an equal probability of heads and tails when freely tossed, will, in the course of a long series of such tosses, create a number of sporadic patterns in which several consecutive heads and several consecutive tails come up.

Dice and other games of chance exhibit similar streaks. A player will suddenly make pass after pass and the game gets "hot." At other times, the dice travel about the table quickly as the "pass" line repeatedly loses. Again, an ability to detect, and go with, the flow is one of the most vital factors in the acquisition of big money. Experienced gamblers are sometimes able to sense when the dice are "right" and "wrong," and bet accordingly. Novices who continue to bet more and more heavily against the streak soon find themselves in completely unanticipated difficulties.

Events also produce turning points at important interim tops and bottoms. If you can identify and follow these major trends, you may be able to take extraordinary profits. As Shakespeare put it, "There is a tide in the affairs of men, which, taken at the flood, leads on to fortune; Omitted, all the voyages of their life is bound in shallows and in miseries." Even worse than the failure to participate in a major move, attempts to buck these enormously strong currents can be extremely costly.

If random events, such as coin tossing and dice, run in streaks, so much the more so do events that involve the decisions of a large number of people, and are therefore influenced by psychological factors, especially so-called mob psychology, produce significant streaks of their own. The securities markets provide numerous examples of such phenomena. An index of prices, such as the Dow Jones Industrial Average, may establish a fairly well defined zone of trading over the course of several months or even a few years. Other closely watched patterns include double and triple tops and bottoms, head and shoulders and inverse head and shoulders, certain pennants, flags, triangles, rectangles, breakaway gaps and island reversals.

As the movement of prices break out of these patterns in either direction, they produce signals that first attract the notice of astute traders and investors. Others become aware of the trend at differing points in time. The funds controlled by these people and institutions tend to flow in the direction of the newly established trend. That is to say, if the trend turns bullish, buying will be attracted; a bearish trend will attract selling. Latecomers will usually produce increased pressure in the direction of the trend, culminating in an explosive move as they stampede onto the bandwagon. When everybody has finally clambered aboard, there is nobody left to continue the trend and a trend reversal is already in the making.

At the time a trend is established, some will inevitably be committed on the wrong side of the market. Let's assume you've bought a stock and it declines in price. You don't want to admit you've made a mistake so you continue to hold the stock at a loss and hope the downtrend is only temporary. You may even decide to buy more of it at a lower price, averaging your loss and enabling you to sell the entire holding without a loss if the stock rebounds sufficiently. The stock, however, continues to decline, finally coming to rest at a small fraction of what you paid for the initial lot. You continue to hold for several years at a considerable loss.

In all situations that involve the putting of funds at risk for the purpose of gain, an essential principle involves the preservation of capital by limiting any possible loss. In securities transactions, this limit (as well as the profit objective) is best decided in advance, long before adverse price action can affect your emotions and cloud your judgment. I recommend the following technique as an aid to breaking the hold a loss may have on you. Simply do not close out your position at the same brokerage house at which you opened it. Buy the security at one house, have it delivered to you in street name (that is, without the necessity of registering the stock in your name) if you are in a hurry to get it. When you decide to sell the security, do so at a profit or a loss in your account at another firm.

The buying and selling brokers need never know whether you took a profit or a loss. The "shame" or "loss of face" millions of normal people feel when they take securities losses of which their brokers are aware, and which needlessly keeps them locked in positions at mounting losses, is thus eliminated, freeing them to move to protect themselves intelligently in response to the market, without regard to this needless emotional attachment. The original buying and selling objectives may then be followed. For those who wish to trade on margin, when the fully paid for security is delivered to the second house, the one at which you intend to sell it, you may request the full margin allowance, deposit the check, and commit these funds at the first brokerage house, or simply make the second purchase at the second house, planning to sell it later through a different firm.

There are many widely differing forms of speculation and each "game" has its own rules of play, its own speed and intensity, its jargon and paraphernalia, its broad mix of players, its history and its characteristic risks and rewards. Not every game is for every player. If you are considering putting funds at risk, you will materially improve your chances of amassing serious gains by carefully selecting the game most compatible, not only with your objectives, but of even greater importance, with your character, temperament and personality.

In the stock market, for example, the same advice followed at the same time by several people will ultimately produce losses for some and profits for others that may

range from minimal to handsome. It is extremely important to understand and appreciate this paradoxical phenomenon that some will profit while others lose even on
the identical commitment undertaken at the same moment. This has been a fact in the stock market for genera-
tions. I witnessed it at close range in the handling of
hundreds of accounts for almost a decade. Profits and
losses are not automatic, depending upon your original
purchase (or short sale) and its timing. Profits "don't just
happen." There are interactions between and among the
players and the playing environment in the stock market
as there are in every other money-seeking venture involving risk, and the combinations have to work well in order
to produce good results. It is like a pianist and a piano;
both have to be "on" to produce good music, As a violin
won't give you a pleasing piano concerto, neither will an
untuned piano or a bad player. It is only when every tum-
bler of the lock falls into place that the door may swing
open to your slightest touch.

Another reason for trading with different brokers (playing in different environments) is that you are likely to find
a significant, apparently unaccountable, difference in the
profitability of your accounts, even after you factor in and
properly weigh time, money and risk against total net gain.
Without rancor, simply discontinue playing the game with
your least profitable brokers, and if you wish to continue
playing this particular game, trade with those with whom
your accounts do best. This is not to imply there is anything necessarily wrong with the brokers with whom you
stop trading, or with their firms. They may even do well
for other clients. It is of secondary importance why trading
with these brokers isn't very profitable.

You may not be able to discover the precise differences
between natural and synthetic vitamins, for example, but
if the natural product produces good results for you which
the synthetic does not, would you not be well advised to

buy the natural? It is an impersonal, practical decision, like avoiding blackjack dealers at whose tables you lost and seeking out dealers you were able to beat. The former may not have cheated you, but it's certainly reasonable to assume the latter didn't either and more prudent to play against the latter if you're playing to win. The latter is a professional dealer playing under the advantage and protections of the house. There is nothing unsporting about eliminating other factors that might be producing losses for you.

In the same way, if you lose three or four consecutive times (at any game that involves risk management) you are at the wrong table, in the wrong casino, or simply not yet prepared to play this game. Stop playing. Make it a rule not to try to make up all of your losses by overcommitting your funds. It is when things are going your way that you may want to raise the stakes, not when you're suffering reverses.

There are many ways to speculate and each offers innumerable opportunities for gain. Therefore, there is no need to rush into any speculative situation prematurely. In fact, any attempt to transfer time pressure to you from any source should signal you not to enter the game. Before attempting to accumulate serious money by speculating you must first determine whether speculation itself is for you and, if so, which is your best game. Your attitude and approach and style of play (that is to say, how well you play the game) are determinative of the results you will achieve in speculating, not, as generally thought, the particular merits of this or that opportunity. This explains why some people of your acquaintance never seem to turn a profit, while others manage to click off one after another, sometimes even on the same vehicle that threw a different rider.

The determination of which game(s) is (are) most suitable for you and where and with whom to play is a time-consuming, painstaking, but necessary process if you are a serious player. As you would not match an inexperienced but promising club player against a champion, you should not place your money at risk among the pros until you have some understanding of, and feeling for, the game. Virtually every game has its lore and its "literature." This material is rather accessible and any serious speculator is well advised to become schooled in the best available printed thinking about his or her prospective game. Biases, both pro and con, self-promotion and publicity for the game itself or any of its playing fields, must be heavily discounted, of course.

After you have studied the game at a distance, if it still attracts you, you should observe it in action before playing. Become aware of the variations in house rules, and the differences in the competence and attitude of their personnel. Greed, dishonesty, sloppiness, or the disinclination to correct their own errors on the part of your money handlers or their employers will cost you dearly and most of the time you won't be aware of it unless you are sensitive, knowledgeable and alert.

In choosing a securities broker, you would look for a well-financed, profitable brokerage house of excellent reputation and house rules that were not unfavorable to the kinds of positions you planned to take. Your customer's broker should be experienced, accurate, reliable, honest, knowledgeable, trained and successful. He or she should not attempt to induce you to overtrade or pretend to have some secret source of inside information. He or she should be available to you during trading hours and should spend some additional time keeping informed. Your broker should also be willing and able to inform you of breaking news, as well as unusual activity, in your prospective and actual holdings. I would also recommend a broker who is not a relative or a close friend.

On entering a new game you should realize that you are

unseasoned, not sure of your strengths and weaknesses, not certain, in fact, whether this game were right for you but willing to find out at limited risk and on a small scale. You would want to enter the game when conditions were favorable and with an upside and downside objective in mind. Let's say, for example, in the stock market, you might be willing to risk a loss of no more than 20 percent (plus commissions) and expect to take a profit of 50 percent (minus commissions) on your first stock trade. Later, when and if you get the feel of this game and decide it's for you, you may decide to raise your profit objectives.

If speculation is your bent, keep the price you pay for learning the game under control. Don't let this "tuition" cost so erode your capital that you're unable to play after you've learned how to do so. If you discover your game and find the rhythm of it, you should be able to produce some winning "streaks." To cite a personal example, I had been speculating in securities and commodities markets for many years when I decided to learn about the opportunities in silver. After much study, I began to play the long side of silver. I traded silver coins, silver bullion, silver coin futures and silver bullion futures rather actively, without a single loss. While I took a skein of trading profits, I maintained a position of 34,992 troy ounces of silver bullion in a Swiss bank. That position yielded a handsome profit. However, had I kept it for the entire joy ride to the top, it would have fetched about $1,750,000, an extraordinary potential gain on a fairly modest total investment.

My record in trading securities and commodities was not particularly distinguished up to the point of the silver trading. I certainly had my share of gains but there were also losses and some were larger than they should have been had I been a better player at the time. What is worth noting is that trading in silver, a game that seemed to require similar skills to those that made for success in the other games I had been playing (with indifferent results), produced only profits.

There is an interaction, a kind of chemistry, that comes into play in speculating that makes even seemingly small differences determinative. As in chemistry itself, even an atom of difference between two molecules may produce strikingly different compounds, so in speculation, the special qualities of each game and the total environment in which it is played produce a context. Each player who becomes immersed in this context produces a slightly different equation, a compound, as it were, of the context and the individual player. It is this "compound," a thing different from the elements that compose it and different as well for each of the players, that works to attract gains and losses.

Had I, for example, traded gold instead of silver, I might have produced an entirely different trading record despite the fact that gold and silver tended to rise and fall in similar patterns and similar skills were needed to trade both markets successfully. Lest this seem unreasonable to readers, the gold and silver markets are similar, not identical; their price movements are also not identical. In addition, the flow of information, including factual data and printed comment, with respect to each metal is different. One is a monetary metal; the other is not and there are scores of other distinctions between the gold and silver markets which might easily have produced dissimilar results. In fact, silver had a much greater percentage of appreciation than gold during this period, and there were potential gains in silver many times greater than in gold.

In considering speculations, I have chosen a number of examples in securities markets, not because there is anything inherently superior about securities as vehicles for profitable speculation but because this form of speculation is familiar to tens of millions of people. If we arbitrarily define as "speculation" a situation that offers opportunities for high rates of return on funds put at risk, we may easily finesse questions as to whether this or that play is a "speculation" or an "investment," the alleged economic usefulness of certain speculative activity, and other such distinctions, and address the more crucial question of how to speculate profitably.

Although I cannot assure or underwrite your profits in any undertaking, I do think there is a useful approach to speculative gains. Most people whose speculative activity I followed professionally for almost a decade never became excellent at any of the speculative "games" they played. They tended to shuttle in and out of several different games, usually at a net loss, not including the value of their time. In addition, they never tried to discover their best game. Bobby Fischer is a great chess player. Pete Rose is a champion baseball player. Pavarotti an outstanding tenor. You would not expect Pete Rose to be a great opera singer or Bobby Fischer a champion baseball player.

The point is obvious. Your best speculative game will produce the biggest profits for you if, indeed, speculation is a game you can play profitably. People with a flair or a talent for a particular game usually demonstrate it long before they become champions. If your early efforts in a speculative game produce three or four consecutive losses, in stocks, for example, this form of play is probably not for you. Stop hurting yourself. The stock market isn't everybody's game. If you are still inclined to speculate, take a rest from actual play, break the losing rhythm, and consider other games. If your early efforts are profitable and you like the game you're in, then take it seriously and try to master it.

You may decline to play a game even if you find it profitable. I once studied an ingenious method for winning at casino blackjack propounded by Dr. Edward O. Thorp and set forth in his brilliant analysis of that game, entitled *Beat the Dealer*. Using a variation of one of his systems, I be-

came a player. Several years ago, en route to the West
Coast on a business trip, a colleague and I spent a couple
of days at a hotel on the strip in Las Vegas. In eleven
sessions of varying lengths, and at relatively low stakes, I
broke even once and won ten times.

Under similar conditions, I think I could win fairly consistently. However, if I decided to play for stakes that
would sufficiently reward the time, money, risk and other
inputs, the conditions would change. Emotional and other
psychological factors would be introduced. If successful, I
would attract the notice of the house(s) and this would
create subtle, and perhaps gross, adverse effects. There is
a world of difference between a mathematical advantage
over the casino and the conversion of this slight edge to
big money. I respect that difference and recognize the fact
that, as a practical matter, high-stake casino gambling is
not my game.

One's speculative game must be profitable and compatible; that is, it must produce gains and be comfortable, feel
right, in so doing. While engaged in the process of discovering your game, stanch the outflow. Stop playing games
that result in losses. "Hunches" and "instinct" can be of
value but don't back yours with serious money until you
are a seasoned and successful player.

Above all, protect yourself against big losses. This is the
single most important element of any sound approach to
the making of big money through speculation. Small
losses cannot hurt you. They should be accepted as part of
the game. In fact, the very basis of many good methods of
speculation involve a means of identifying situations favorable to the player and either a) hazarding more on such
plays and less on the unfavorable plays (as in casino blackjack, for example) so that by winning more of the big bets
and losing more of the small bets, you have a growing net
gain; or, b) putting money at risk only on the favorable
situations, those in which the estimated rewards consid-

erably outweigh the estimated risks (as in the securities markets, for example). Both of these approaches take into account the inevitability of some losses and both attempt to limit the size of these losses.

One technique for avoiding big losses is to divide the amount of money you intend to put at risk into five or six parts and never risk more than one part on a single trade (or session of play, or other speculative venture). If it is possible to preset a maximum possible loss, as in securities trading and casino gambling, you would stop risking any further loss if that point were reached (on a single trade or during a session of play). Don't "average" a loss or increase the amounts you put at risk in order to attempt to overcome losses. If you've been doing something unsuccessfully, don't raise the stakes. This is a common, potentially dangerous, error.

While you're finding and mastering your game, protect your profits by accepting them when the upside limit you preset is reached and never permit a profit of half of this amount to become a loss. Keep records of your play and learn from your successes and failures. Did you violate any rules or principles? How might you have turned in a better performance? If your record is not profitable, you must be willing to accept the likelihood that you have not yet found your game.

Be aware of the cyclical nature of most games so that you may position yourself with the trend after it is established. However, don't anticipate a change in trend as this will work against you during the wild, climactic excesses that often precede the final exhaustion of a trend. You would be well advised not to risk any money until you are fully prepared, have studied the game enough to be able to play it without the guidance and advice of others and after your practice plays have been successful. Then, when you, not your barber or your broker or your brother-in-law, can evaluate a play in which the odds are in your favor in every measurable way and you would not be under a mental, financial or emotional strain to make a limited commitment, you may elect to do so if you consider the play sufficiently attractive in terms of its risks and rewards.

It's difficult to establish blanket rules for holding your position applicable to all games, but here are some suggestions. Until you become a successful, seasoned player, you would hold your position, in general, until conditions changed to the point that reevaluation indicated your play were no longer justified, or your preset upside or downside limits were breached. When you become successful and experienced, you may wish to try for even greater profits. If you were in a game that permitted you to cash in your position at will, once you were halfway to your upside objective, you would change your downside limit to the break-even point. You would remain sensitive to changing conditions. In casino blackjack, for example, if a new dealer entered the game and the house began to get "lucky," this would constitute a sufficient change of conditions to stop my play and to cause me to avoid that dealer.

Whether and when to increase your commitment is a highly personal matter. Nevertheless, I offer the following guidelines. Never raise the stakes of a losing speculation or do so after you have taken several losses. You may raise, if comfortable for you, when things are going your way. In committing additional funds to a position (like securities) the new additions should be progressively smaller, so that your original position is analogous to the base of a pyramid. This method of accumulation protects the profit you have in the original position from adverse action. A small move against your interest would not be able to cancel your profit on the entire position. Don't overcommit your funds and don't play too often. Unless you are in the business of speculating, you should be playing selectively, when the measurable factors are favorable. There should be periods when you are on the sidelines and your funds are not at risk.

The time to fold is when your downside limit is breached or when supervening conditions make the commitment unattractive or undesirable. If you are relatively inexperienced, you may be content to cash in your holdings when your preset upside objective is reached or approached. If you are experienced and have a successful record in a particular game, you may want to consider whether a play has the potential of a long, arching move to super profits.

The time to walk away is when you realize the game is not for you by virtue of a number of consecutive losses, a generally unprofitable record of speculating in the game, or a loss of interest in, or attraction to, the game for any reason. You may remain open to the possibility of finding some other form of speculation, if you wish. You would also do well to walk away from strong sales pitches or any other pressure to draw you into a commitment. If you don't sufficiently understand the game or you are not completely prepared to play it, if you are in doubt, if you don't like the game or the players, if the gyrations of the game become wild or erratic, if the minimum amount of money involved is uncomfortably high for you or any loss would be a strain, I suggest you do not enter the game or leave it at your early convenience.

Tens of billions of dollars are made and lost each year on speculative ventures of one kind or another in this country alone. Most players have little understanding of the speculative games in which they hazard their money and lack a cohesive approach to speculating. Not surprisingly, many lose more than they can afford. However, not all speculations are wild gambles. Indeed, some offer extremely attractive odds to those who are willing to learn well the games in which they would put their money at risk before they do so, to adopt a rational and disciplined approach to speculative opportunities and to remain vigilant while keeping open to improving their performance.

XIII

The Information Game

We live in a communications context fueled by "information." Without reliable information, effective decision-making is impossible. The information we receive is composed of thoughts, feelings, facts, knowledge, opinions, vibes, beliefs, or some combination thereof. It may be clear or fuzzy, true or false, distorted, incomplete, garbled or staged. On the basis of information, wars have been won and lost, governments installed and toppled, and fortunes created and squandered. Indeed, the giving, shaping and withholding of information plays a pivotal role in every sector of human enterprise. The total resources currently committed to the acquisition, processing and distribution of information in all forms is incalculable and rising. No less than several billions of dollars and hundreds of millions of person-hours are allocated each week to the gathering, organization, storage, dissemination and consumption of information in this country alone. Many giant corporations and thousands of smaller ones engage in it exclusively. Other companies, including a number of multinational conglomerates, have major "information" divisions. Information is so important and so pervasive in our society that all forms of business organizations have

149

t in the production, distribution and/or con-
of it.

us plays several roles in the total intake and
outuov f information. Not only in your economic life, but
in your private roles as well, you are a kind of information
reception, storage, retrieval, processing, production, dissemination and consumption center. How you perform
these functions directly affects your net worth. You may
be intelligent and personable and do your job well but if
you don't gather information well and use it effectively,
you won't know how to manage yourself to your optimum
advantage and your progress will be limited. Without a
conceptual understanding of the importance of information and the development of the skills required to play the
information game at least competently, you will not develop the overview or the perspective with which to get
beyond the immediate situation to a major objective.

A product and a service, information has many fascinating properties. Properly utilized, it is an invaluable asset
and a multipurpose tool for facilitating the magic of thinking rich. In fact, thousands of individuals have learned
how to convert information to cash with felicitous regularity. Millions of others are aware that such a conversion
process takes place but the entry points to this rich mine
remain frustratingly inaccessible to them. The information
these people receive and disseminate is of too poor an ore
to be converted to cash. It is stale and unmagical, either
arriving too late or too distorted to be of money-making
value.

How, then, may you shovel through the heavy tonnage
of informational debris that surrounds you, the thick slurry
of thoughts, feelings, facts, headlines, allegations, guesti-
mates, beliefs, vibes, biases, puffery, fuzz, garble, distortion, commentary, publicity plant and evasion, to find a
lode of sufficient economic value to be worth mining? The
first step is to stop putting yourself through one informational maze after another. If the information you've been

receiving for years (and passing along to others) isn't of value, is it not time to curtail your intake from these sources and develop others? In addition, until you're well along toward omniscience, would you not be helping yourself and others if you resolved to stop sharing not only obviously bad information, but *all* information that might affect other people's money unless you are prepared to guarantee their possible losses?

Once you have gratuitously involved other people's money with your advice, you not only stand to incur the fallout that follows their losses (and some losses are almost inevitable), but your own freedom of action and clarity of thought with respect to that advice are affected. For example, in an expansive mood and with the best intentions, if you suggest that somebody invest money in a stock you recently purchased, and the stock begins to decline (after they buy it), whereas you might ordinarily limit your risk by taking a small loss, you are reluctant to do so because you will feel obliged to inform the other person and you don't want to suggest a loss for him or her. The result may be that both you and your friend continue to hold the stock and subsequently you both take a big loss. Sharing bad information is a sign of unenlightenment, not of generosity. The Zen statement that those who know don't talk; those who talk don't know, is well observed.

Any serious analyses of how information reaches you, how you process and organize it, the specific short-term and cumulative effects it produces on you, and the ways in which you impart information to others, fascinating and largely unexplored territory, lie outside the scope of this work. My purpose in examining information is much more modest. It is to effect a framework in which you may receive, organize, store and utilize information profitably, and to help you avoid the losses inherent in "bad" information. In doing so, the focus will be on quality, timing, importance and penetration.

In evaluating the quality of information, its source is of

obvious importance. How close is your source to the actual or primary source of the information, its point of origin? The best-intentioned secondary sources of information are usually only repeating their version of what they received from another secondary source. If you've ever watched a short joke told in one language to an individual who, in turn, tells it in another language to a third person, and so on, you are no doubt aware that after about a half dozen such translations, when the last person to hear the joke finally re-translates it into the original language, less than five minutes later, it is garbled beyond recognition. A group of well-meaning, disinterested people motivated to do their best to relay the information intact, renders a short statement utterly meaningless in short order.

Nor is the source of your information always reliable. If you receive information from a secondary source it is difficult, if not impossible, to determine its reliability, even assuming your source is reliable and is transmitting precisely what was received. Your source gets information from still another source, as does that source, and so on. Like water flowing into a sea, once information passes a certain point it is difficult to determine where it originated and its original quality.

Is the information verifiable? Can it be independenly checked or can any hard evidence be adduced to support it? Is the primary source named or unnamed? In short, is there anything you can do to assure the accuracy of the information or must you accept it on faith or reject it? The information may simply be false. For example, I once saw an unscrupulous customers' broker create "inside information." When an important item was printed on the Dow Jones news ticker (often accompanied by a bell to signify its special nature), this man would rush to the order desk and place an order either to buy a couple of hundred shares of the affected security, or to sell short a like amount, at the market, depending upon his evaluation of the effect of the news.

When he began this practice, he would omit the name and account number the order required but the order department demurred. He countered by putting an unsuspecting customer's account number on the order, one who had either given him certain discretion over his or her account or who was somebody the customer's broker knew would accept the trade. The account number, however, did not correspond with the name of the account he wrote on the order. The name was that of somebody who had an account in which the broker had an interest.

Having selected only those items of news which were of special importance and which were likely to produce an immediate move in the security involved, if he guessed right he would change the account number on the order, conforming it to the name, an account in which he participated. If he guessed wrong and the stock were selling off, he would leave the order as written, as he knew the account number would control the trade and place the loss in the customer's account. But how to make the loss acceptable?

This is where he created "inside information." He would call the client, tell him that his "friend downtown" had informed the broker earlier in the day that "such-and-such," and here he would insert the gist of the news item. The broker realized that the client would want to participate in the advantage of this "advance" information (and remember the information is important and its superficial significance was strong enough to interest the customer's broker to buy the affected security or sell it short). Therefore, the broker would continue, he bought (or sold short) a couple of hundred shares for the client. He emphasizes the "source's" alleged infallibility by telling the client that a few minutes ago, the announcement appeared on the news ticker and, of course, the "source" was exactly right again. He ends by cautioning the client against worrying if the stocks reacts in the wrong direction initially as it is only a temporary condition and reminds him or her that

not everybody is given access to such "inside information."

Obviously, sources of information like this broker are
not unbiased. Advertisers, promoters, public relations people, salespeople and advocates of all descriptions create a
great deal of information which, if not entirely false, as in
the case of the unscrupulous broker, is often considerably
less than the whole truth. These people are not paid to
disclose the weak points of their clients or the goods and/
or services in which their clients deal. Euphemisms, puff,
half-truths, and scores of other communications techniques create blizzards of unreliable data to which we are
all exposed. Whether it is our vote, our attention or the
way we spend or invest our money that is being solicited,
there are few of any age who have not succumbed to this
confetti. In fact, admissions against interest are so unusual
they are properly regarded as having special credibility.

As information confected to advance an interest other
than yours travels from its original source en route to you
it is relayed from one person, place or thing to another,
becoming distorted by inevitable additions, deletions, al-
terations and embroideries of many varieties. It is not uncommon for some of the relayers to assign themselves a
greater role than the facts support in the process of impart-
ing the information to you. Casual onlookers or even
overhearers may be transfigured into principal players; the
merest of acquaintances involved in the passage of the
information become close, personal friends, and there is a
tendency to place the relayer closer and closer to the
source of the information than the facts justify. The longer
it takes and the greater number of scrims and psyches
through which it must pass before it reaches you, the more
impurities the stream of information is likely to include.
Once these messages are thus adulterated, no magic alem-
bic can distill and purify them. Like the translated and
retranslated story referred to earlier, the effluent that

emerges from these channels of communication are, at best, hopelessly garbled and unfit for your consumption.

In addition to the indecipherably distorted, the intentionally false, and the amateur and professional advocacy, there is another major source of unreliable information often called scuttlebutt. Part rumor, part gossip, scuttlebutt is usually fueled by the needs and/or desires of those who engage in it to appear close to important sources of information and/or power. The passing along of bits of information about big deals, important impending changes in a particular power structure, the foibles and peccadilloes of others, especially the wealthy, powerful and/or celebrated, and other expressly or implicitly restricted information confers, at least momentarily, an enhanced status on those who traffic in such scuttlebutt. Some use scuttlebutt as counterfeit currency with which to repay a debt of gratitude or create an obligation. Others may simply wish to be of service by sharing the latest hearsay.

Despite an occasional useful piece of information, the sources we have so far considered provide information much too unreliable to be utilized as a means of conversion to money. If you accept this view or if you are willing to recall some of the painful, needless losses these sources were instrumental in introducing into your life, I suggest you resolve not to permit any of these sources to harm you ever again by influencing your management of money. You should also be willing to stop any further transmission of information from these sources.

In discouraging tipsters, advisers and other self-appointed managers of my money (whether motivated by the lure of a commission, fee, share of the profits, or simply the desire to provide a life of wealth and luxury for me) I have found it useful to explain that I am not disposed to act on information, the initial source of which is unknown or unreachable, information that doesn't allow for independent verification and crosscheck, or information that is simply an invitation to follow the action or advice of some-body else without providing a basis for so doing other than that Mr. Big or Ms. X, who is allegedly always right, or some such, is allegedly doing thus and so.

I don't mind making my own mistakes because I can learn from them but all I can learn from other people's errors is not to attempt to follow others, which I already know without having to make each costly mistake. Ergo, pass. People who provide bad information do so regularly and repeatedly, if unchecked. You have a right, I would say an obligation, to be vigilant and rigorous, to ask questions, to scrutinize answers. Don't be a passive receiver of bad information. Those who can provide valuable in-formation are high-density people who do so rarely and discriminately. The most successful players of the information game have learned to treat information with care and to manage their intake, storage, use and outflow of information with discretion.

Unreliable information usually requires your complicity to be damaging. Similarly, potentially valuable informa-tion is only a raw material that can be put to good use or wasted. Certain bits of information can only be acquired by personally assembling and organizing them. This di-rect, personal connection adds a strength and a solidity on which you can rely and from which you can profit. The precise contents of your information system will differ from mine but the approach will probably be similar. Al-though some individuals and organizations spend large sums on personnel and equipment, there are effective sys-tems you can develop for yourself at virtually no cost.

The basic tools are an ordinary Rolodex, Wheeldex or similar set of cards (I recommend the large size), a number of manila file folders, a desk calendar and one or more filing cabinets. The latter is desirable but not essential. Properly kept, the cards, the folders and the calendar pro-vide the simplest and most economical system I know of

for developing, storing and retrieving information. Elabo-
rate filing systems that make retrieval complicated soon
become little more than storage bins. They are rarely consulted and tend to become useless, even unreliable.

The cards should be arranged alphabetically by both individual and company name, providing a simple cross-
reference, as each company card would include all the
names among your cards employed by the company. The
cards would contain the home and business addresses,
telephone numbers (including direct dialing numbers), bi-
ographical data, taste preferences, schools attended, club
memberships, dates of incoming and outgoing calls and
other communications, dates and places of meetings,
impressions, names of secretary, spouse, children and sib-
lings, if any, and their nicknames, if any, cyclical data,
observations and any other additional data you care to include.

These data would be updated continually and without
asking the subject a lot of questions. Include cards for people you don't know (but may have heard or read about in
trade publications). The cards should also list those to
whom this person reports and who report to this person.

There should be a file folder, arranged alphabetically,
for each person, company and project with whom and with
which you are involved in a profit-oriented way. The information on the cards should be integrated into the table
of organization of each company among your folders. An
understanding of how the power flows in a company is
important for several reasons. As a customer, it allows you
to reach a level of personnel that can put matters right for
you and leave ample room for assistance from above, if
necessary. A reference to a person two levels above sometimes produces magical results, especially if you use the
nickname, but be sure to use the nickname correctly. If the
person's name is Leonard, his nickname might be Len,
Lenny, Linc, Bud, Leo, Lee, Leon, Chip, Skip, Sonny or

Tex. The correct nickname will sound right and may be effective but if you get it wrong, you will lose much credibility.

If you would like to establish a profit-oriented relationship with a company, it is most helpful to be able to deal directly with people who have the authority to implement your plans and projects. Only a handful of people in the company have the authority to commit serious money; all others can only veto or recommend. The more levels of personnel your project has to pass through, the more likely it is to be rejected before it reaches the person who could have implemented it, and the more attenuated its presentation is likely to be by people who are farther and farther from the person down the line to whom you spoke. The table of organization will show you at a glance how the lines of power are constructed. You may then develop an intelligent approach to a person who can say yes instead of no or maybe.

By keeping abreast of developments in your fields of interest through trade publications and other reliable sources, you may construct and update tables of organization of companies in these fields and add cards for the principal players. As the latter move from job title to job title and company to company, you would update your files but retain all of the outdated information. Retaining the outdated information multiplies the probabilities that you can locate somebody you know well enough to effect a personal introduction, if desired, to the person whose card you are keeping but have never met.

The calendar would provide a useful list of all appointments, meetings, incoming and outgoing calls, lunches, breakfasts, dinners, impressions, notes, etcetera. Each page would be collected and stored in a single envelope for the calendar or fiscal year. In addition to a chronological record, the calendar pages are good evidence for tax purposes, if needed.

The three tools (cards, folders and calendar) are inter-related and easily kept up to date. They are wieldy and relatively compact and storage and retrieval are uncomplicated. Keeping such files will help develop certain inter-relationships which might otherwise remain undetected. Topics of interest, companies, and people with whom you deal or wish to deal may be conveniently tracked. You may more easily pick up the rhythms of people and events, detect trends and changes of trends, power shifts and alliances. Even your own health cycles may be followed by logging calls and visits to doctors on their cards. You should begin to get a heightened sense of the interconnectedness of people and events and their relationships to fields of special interest to you. You may discover that the rains in Maine have a direct effect on the price of potatoes in New York.

Learn to be resourceful in seeking out sources of information. You can sometimes get an excellent feel for a securities investment by speaking directly with the company president or other well-placed company executives. Corporate officers are not permitted to give out inside information prematurely but I have gotten valuable clues to timing from voice tones, pauses, a few specifics and some general observations by calling on a Saturday or after normal business hours and dialing past the switchboard directly to the executive's desk.

A call every few weeks plus some follow-ups with the person in charge of corporate stockholder relations, the comptroller and the financial vice-president keeps me surprisingly well informed. Ask your stockbroker what information might be useful if you are in doubt. Learn the patois of the business and try to speak intelligently in the language of the annual report or the trade in general. Inside information, after all, comes from insiders and I like to develop my own direct sources. Learn the rhythms of the players and look for inconsistencies in the information you get from the various people who are in a position to know the facts.

You can develop other primary sources of information by joining organizations in fields that interest you. The low-density people in the group can supply the gossip and rumor that will help you identify the high-density people. The closer you are to reliable primary sources, the earlier in the cycle, the less distorted the information is likely to be.

Some secondary sources may also be of value. Libraries can supply a great deal of information and a well-trained, helpful librarian can be an invaluable aide. In addition to public libraries, there are private, specialized, college and university and other libraries, all or parts of which are likely to be accessible to you at no charge or for a modest fee. Many fields of interest cut across national boundaries. The best sources should have information available on a worldwide basis in order to keep you fully informed.

If you need to follow a specific topic of interest closely, there are clipping services with which you can arrange to receive published articles for an agreed period of time for a fee. Some of these services provide worldwide coverage. A good librarian may be helpful in directing your inquiries.

Information, like any other resource, can be managed well or poorly. Without reliable information, effective decision-making is impossible. Most people receive a mix of information of uncertain quality at a point in time well into its distribution cycle. With inadequate means of evaluating this thin gruel and virtually no reliable techniques for refining the mass and extracting what little value it might contain, no effective storage or retrieval, and no system for updating and improving their intake, it is not surprising the welter of data is largely useless, unproductive, even damaging. On the other hand, those who realize the importance of creating and developing reliable primary and secondary sources of information and learn to use them to good advantage, reap the rewards reserved for the accomplished players of the information game.

XIV

Your Kitchen Cabinet

A basic purpose of this work, and one that pervades much of it, is to encourage your thought and action in the direction of organizing and developing the resources you need in order to function as a primary power source. From your will, knowledge, ability and energy, all else follows. A lack of will, knowledge, ability or energy involves you in a network of dependency and restricted choices. Dependency and restricted choices narrow the very aperture of life itself and produce a long train of unfulfilling consequences. By exercising choices and making the decisions that affect your life, you take dominion over yourself, you become the chief executive of your own life, not simply the person who carries out the dictates of somebody else or of necessity.

Many people attempt to function by going to this or that person for advice and guidance in the "clutch of circumstance," putting the jagged pieces of an incomplete or broken puzzle before them in the hope of assistance. This method is not designed to produce the best results. I suggest the assembling of a highly skilled team, the members of which you have carefully selected in advance, so that when you are ready to present something for their consideration, they will be able to help effectuate your purpose. This is the primary function of your kitchen cabinet.

The expression "kitchen cabinet" has two rather different meanings: a) a cupboard built into a kitchen used for the storage of dishes, silverware and/or canned goods and the like, and b) a group of unofficial advisers, usually to a president or other head of government. It is an extension of the latter meaning that is the subject of this chapter. Your kitchen cabinet, in this context, refers to a number of specially selected people (and other aids) you may call upon either individually or in various combinations for the purpose of consultation, assistance, advice, and/or the implementation of your ideas, plans and projects.

Ours is a mostly service economy but the quality of service is so uneven that strategies designed to assure excellence are mandatory. Ideally, the individuals in your kitchen cabinet are high-density people who may be experts, specialists or professionals, but regardless of their particular field of interest, they are competent and reliable and they have a track record of accomplishment; they know how to get things done. They will act as your personal wealth facilitators and you will, in all likelihood, find them only after a diligent talent search and much sifting. Your ability to assemble a first-class kitchen cabinet is important, perhaps crucial, for, although good advice is not always easy to obtain and it may be expensive, bad advice is usually much more costly.

The precise composition of your kitchen cabinet will reflect your own interests but there are some general guidelines. Mine, for example, consists of a number of professional specialists and generalists, some other experts, friends and associates, plus some of the best services I need with a high degree of regularity, all carefully selected and kitchen-tested in the real world where some of the more gristled veterans have performed nobly and brilliantly. Some of the relationships are reciprocal; often, fees and/or participatory shares are involved, but regardless of the specific financial arrangements (or their absence), the mechanism is effective.

Superb health care is not always available on demand. There are a number of personal, idiosynchratic factors that go into my own selections of doctors and I recommend advance planning and some trial and error in order that you find the best personal matchups. A first-rate internist, family doctor or general practitioner is about as important to health care as a first-string quarterback to a professional football team. In addition to excellent credentials and training, I prefer a doctor who is forthright in telling me what he or she thinks; is associated with an extremely well-equipped and well-staffed hospital, one that is relatively convenient to my family and others who would be concerned if I were in the hospital, and more than likely a teaching hospital; and a practitioner who seems to take a personal interest in my well-being. The point about the hospital's convenience to those who would be visiting me is more important than may be apparent, as personal visits and questions asked by those close to the patient are important in keeping the hospital at a high delivery level of care for the patient. The colleagues of my doctor affiliated with this kind of hospital will most likely be outstanding specialists and will be available to me via referral, if needed. If I am later hospitalized on the recommendation of one of these specialists, it will be at this well-staffed and equipped hospital and my general doctor will have privileges at his or her own hospital. I would want my general doctor to be old enough to be seasoned and experienced but sufficiently energetic and interested in keeping up with current medical developments and to be open to them. I also prefer a depth of background in the field that goes beyond minimal standards. My internist, for example, is also a Ph.D. in pharmacology; my ophthalmologist is also a skilled surgeon, and so on.

A good legal adviser is of obvious importance. However,

no one attorney is likely to be your best choice to handle the entire gamut of your legal matters. I avoid lawyers who speak in absolutes, especially negative ones ("Impossible"; "Forget it"; "No way"). This kind of speech connotes lazy, sloppy thinking in a lawyer, not the kind of mentality you would expect to provide quality work. Procrastination, a characteristic built into our legal system and many of its practitioners, should likewise be avoided. It isn't reasonable for you to expect to preempt the schedule of busy professionals but if the latter fail to keep time commitments and the explanations are unconvincing and even unvolunteered, you're probably dealing with a procrastinator. Adjournments, postponements, continuances and other delays are part of the stock in trade of attorneys, not as aids to their clients or the general welfare, but as expedients for themselves and judges. Other things being equal, the more cases a lawyer takes on, the greater his or her income. However, the more cases in the file, the less time may be allotted to each one. The result is delay, congestion and frustration for the client.

In order to avoid such procrastinators and to employ professionals who respect the clock and the calendar, it helps to begin at the beginning. It isn't a good idea to put yourself into the hands of a professional like a great mass of wet clay and hope that all will go well. Ask for dates and deadlines and react if they're not observed. Ask for copies of the work product to be routinely sent to you as it progresses. Keep records in a file of your own and on your Rolodex as to appointments and deadlines kept, missed and canceled and calls not returned promptly or at all. State your requirements in this regard at the outset. If these understandings are not met and you have reason to be dissatisfied, discuss these feelings with the professional. If there is no radical improvement, you may be much better off with a more responsive and responsible professional. Professional procrastinators don't suddenly reform.

If you need a professional specialist, the best one you

can afford in relation to the importance of the matter, is usually the right approach. Too often, a non-specialist or less than a distinguished specialist is learning at your expense. You will be billed for this needlessly spent time and you may expect to get considerably less than excellence for your money.

The legal profession has become so highly specialized that the single practitioner, the professional who works alone, and who cannot know every ramification of every matter, is often at a disadvantage. If a wealthy client, for example, presents a matrimonial matter, the best legal advice would include an analysis of the tax consequences to the client and the members of his or her family. The individual practitioner, even if well versed in the field of matrimonial law as such, is unlikely to keep abreast of all the continually shifting and changing refinements of taxation, a separate specialty. Even the most conscientious, energetic and diligent professionals cannot be at the top of their form in all areas of the law.

I think the team approach (group practice, partnership, and so on) to the practice of law better serves the practitioner and the client. If the lawyer handling your matrimonial matter were a member of a law partnership, one of whose members were a tax expert, you would be likely to get a better result for your money. There is an additional bonus in that first-class professionals may be expected to be unwilling to form partnerships with mediocre colleagues. You derive the benefits of having, in effect, a practitioner of excellence screening and selecting other such professionals and bestowing his or her seal of approval on a colleague in the strongest terms. A good lawyer in your kitchen cabinet who is a member of a partnership or other legal team thus provides access to a broad range of legal services.

Although an increasing number of doctors are sharing suites of offices, in-house laboratory facilities, equipment and technicians, this approach to the practice of medicine is not yet widespread enough to give most people the best medical care available. Doctors in this country have not formed enough teams across medical specialties to make this approach practical. However, the best staffed and equipped teaching hospitals convenient to you may be looked upon as part of your medical team, as was suggested earlier. By selecting any doctor associated with such an excellent facility, you gain access to all of the other doctors associated with the hospital, and, of course, to the hospital itself. Your doctor is likely to recommend his or her hospital colleagues as your medical specialists and, again, the best hospitals may be expected to be selective in choosing staff and affiliations. I would also choose a dentist, ophthalmologist and other health professionals such as, for example, a pediatrician, gynecologist, and so on, if needed, with similar care.

The quality of professional service is extremely uneven in major urban centers. If you appreciate professional excellence, are aware of the great disparity in the results you may reasonably anticipate in all but the most routine matters, depending upon the quality of the services employed on your behalf, and good results are important to you, you will not mind being on the qui vive for effective professionals you are likely to need to consult. Ask high-density people you know well to make recommendations. Competent professionals may be able to direct you to other competent professionals in fields outside of their own. A good lawyer may know of a first-rate doctor, a competent doctor may be able to recommend an excellent accountant, and so on. The reason I suggest the recommendation be outside the profession of the recommender is that it eliminates the possibility, however unlikely, that referral fees, also known as fee-splitting (a practice not uncommon within the same profession but almost unheard of across professions), will influence the recommendation.

There are specialties within professional specialties and you should be careful to stay within the area of special competence of the professional if you expect to receive optimum benefits. Tax advice, for example, involves a number of separate areas of specialty. One involves the handling of your business and personal tax returns. Another involves tax shelters of various kinds designed to increase your keeping money, both present and future. There is also the matter of estate planning, ways of augmenting your estate and directing it to those you want to benefit, and keeping as much as possible out of the tax collector's net. It is unlikely that a single individual will be able to provide excellent services in all of these areas.

In health care, you may want to consider a number of modalities in addition to orthodox medicine. Medical nutrition, orthomolecular medicine, chiropractic, homeopathic medicine, osteopathy, holistic medicine and other approaches may provide not only corrective care, but preventive and maintenance care designed to keep you at a higher level of health and wellness than merely the absence of obvious clinical symptoms of disease and/or distress.

Depending upon your temperament and attitude, a religious or other spiritual leader or adviser and/or a therapist may be of value in helping to keep you in good balance. A close friend, somebody you have known for several years, and who is familiar with your highs and lows, your temperament, character and judgment and who is willing to tell you what he or she thinks, the unvarnished truth, even if that view is diametrically opposed to your own, can be an important part of your kitchen cabinet. This person's judgment, even if he or she is not an expert in the particular field under consideration, may provide an important counterweight. Of course, the history of consultation and advice between you and your friend will give you a clue as to what corrective lens, if any (from your own point of view) you need to put in place in order to make your friend's opinion more useful. As with a bridge partner with whom you've played for years, you learn to crank in the style of the player in evaluating the bid. In addition, one or two close friends in your own field would obviously be helpful in exchanging reliable information and comparing notes.

The best group of advisers and implementers is assembled slowly and carefully, long before the need is urgent and, in fact, in anticipation of recurrent and/or expected needs. In addition to the members already considered, you may want to include an insurance expert, a knowledgeable travel agent, an honest and capable stockbroker, a couple of bankers, and probably a good real estate broker. A thorough talent search for these people will pay big and continuing dividends in terms of the results you may expect and the handling you will receive. High-density people will be able to provide leads to this talent and you should be willing to reciprocate by occasionally making your own recommendations if you know of unusually able talent. Don't try to take shortcuts by accepting an entire block of talent from one or two sources. This can sometimes produce an inbred point of view, divided loyalties, or even breaches of confidence.

Regardless of their particular field, part of the inventory of all service people is their time. You must respect their time if you are to have a good relationship with them. Don't break appointments if you can possibly keep them. Be punctual to meetings with them. Don't waste time by rambling or straying from the subject. If documents are needed, have copies with you. Don't needlessly prolong the visit. Be specific and come to the point directly. Focus. Help them to help you. Be responsive to their good ideas and suggestions. Try to set a date, even if tentative, for the completion of whatever they are going to do for you. This is how they may respect your time. Pay their bills promptly and include a personal note. When telephoning, have a written list of what you want to discuss so that the conversation is brief but productive. Return their calls and other communications as soon as you can. This creates a lively tempo and a good working relationship. They also appreciate high-density clients.

Of less than kitchen cabinet rank, perhaps, but nevertheless important, are a number of other service people who, by simply doing their job especially well can expedite and facilitate a project of yours but who, if less than excellent, can needlessly snarl the best-conceived plan. A good example of this is a messenger service. If the service is inefficient, inconsiderate, dawdling, or otherwise of unacceptable quality, your envelope or parcel, the contents of which may have taken you months to assemble in their current flawless form, may be gathering foodstains in a luncheonette instead of being transformed by its addressee into a golden goose, while time runs out.

A first-rate barber or hairstylist is an asset and is worth shopping for until you find somebody excellent. There is a vast difference between basic competence sufficient to become licensed, and excellence. You may have the latter for a small price differential (if any) in any medium or large urban area of the country if you look for it. The styling of your hair probably makes the greatest difference in your appearance for the fewest dollars and it is a mistake to keep going back to the same people who consistently send you out of the shop looking considerably less than your best. Similarly, a tailor or dressmaker who has taste, ability, and a sense of professionalism about keeping commitments, is worth seeking out and adding to your talent roster.

Note that these people are not on your payroll, not part of your full-time staff. They are simply available to you when, as and if needed and they can be assembled and activated virtually at will. They add depth to your resources. In this category I would include good temporary employees. For example, if you do not employ a household staff, you would do well to look at services that supply butlers, maids, bartenders and the like and line up the best before you experiment at the wrong time. A couple of tries on occasions of lesser importance should yield a service on which you may rely and you may well be able to reserve the specific individuals you found praiseworthy if you make the arrangements early enough. Secretaries, stenographers, typists and other office personnel are also available on a temporary, part-time, or one-shot basis.

Professional, service-oriented librarians can be of great help in directing you to valuable sources of specialized information, including translations of publications from reliable worldwide sources. Good business equipment and office supplies are recommended. Your business and personal stationery represent you and you may have the best quality at a relatively insignificant additional cost. Even a clean typeface and a new ribbon make a difference.

It isn't always easy to distinguish the gifted, the service-oriented, the unusually competent and the most compatible people from their second-rate counterparts, especially before they have performed a job or completed work for you. However, if you have been or will be involving yourself, on one basis or another, with any of the elements of what I refer to as your kitchen cabinet, that is, the people, places and things that can facilitate the magic of thinking rich for you (or hamper your progress), and you accept the premise that how good these facilitators are and how well they work for you are important to your success and well-being, you should be willing to choose these elements with great care. The best time to begin to assemble your kitchen cabinet is long before the need is great. As in solving a jigsaw puzzle, once you put some of the elements together, it becomes easier to assemble the other parts, and as the assemblage takes place, new patterns emerge, new vantage points are presented, which make your progress surer and more secure.

XV

How to Precipitate Money

Rainfall and other familiar forms of precipitation are natural consequences of certain conditions. Money may also be precipitated under conducive conditions you can create. The precipitation of money does not require your becoming a full-time entrepreneur or your investing of large sums of money or the taking of other relatively large risks. In fact, the precipitation of handsome sums of money need not even take much time. A few years ago, for example, a colleague and I, while engaged in separate, unrelated activities, precipitated close to a quarter of a million dollars. It took us a total of about six weeks of work each, if all of the hours of time we expended over a period of about eighteen months were compressed into blocks of time and assembled as workweeks. The time we spent was comprised of irregular segments that ranged from a few minutes up to perhaps four days, including traveling, and did not interfere with our other business interests. More about how we did this later. First, let's look at some of the general principles of money precipitation.

Vast sums of money are being earned repeatedly by a number of so-called middle people, while many times that number spend a great deal more time attempting to close

172

deals that never materialize. By middle people, I mean those who get paid for interconnecting buyers and sellers or, in fact, who supply a missing side of a transaction, whether such people happen to be licensed to do so or not. These middle people include brokers, dealers, agents, representatives, finders, etcetera. There are, to be sure, billions of dollars of transactions in the real world, within the range of your telephones, the postal system, public and private carriers and couriers, and other means of communication and transportation, most of which are accessible to you if you become skilled in reeling these deals into the boat. You will, in all likelihood, come across opportunities for precipitating money, especially if you seek them. Whether or not you are paid for your efforts and if so, how well, depends, in large amount upon how you go about it.

You need not be an expert to be paid well. You may be able to join forces with a knowledgeable middle person and learn all you need to know about the precipitation of money while doing so but you must be able to perform a service. This service typically involves a buyer, a lender or a supplier, but there are other variations. In fact, it is extremely likely you already know people, perhaps your own attorney, for example, who are able to precipitate money and who would be willing to establish a mutually rewarding money-precipitating relationship with you if you approached them with a feasible plan. Few people in our society are averse to making large sums of money legitimately. I would suggest, however, that you avoid alliances with ponderous, greedy and/or procrastinating people and that your agreement be reduced to writing and approved by an attorney whose services you hire for this purpose.

The elements involved in these transactions, as has been suggested, are usually buyers, suppliers, money, closers, entree, contracts and know-how. The common denominator among these elements is people. People are the key, the one indispensable element to your successful precipitation of money.

Middle people are often maligned as unnecessary, even parasitic, persons who are overpaid for doing little or nothing. While this is certainly true in some instances, especially when there are daisy chains of middle people who are dealing with other middle people, not with principals. Middle people, however, may perform an important, even crucial, economic function in putting together viable deals. Competent and creative middle people may even originate deals and shepherd them to fruition.

A bad talent agent may do nothing but sign the talent to a contract and thereafter, for the term of the contract, receive a percentage of the talent's earnings. However, a good agent may perform a number of valuable services for the same percentage of the talent's income. An able literary agent, for example, will submit book proposals to those people who would be most interested in the projects offered, people who would be able to make a financial commitment (or who, at the very least, would be involved in or close to such decisions), will negotiate the terms of contracts, act as a buffer between author and publisher and perform other functions helpful to both the talent and the publisher. A creative literary agent might originate concepts for book projects for talent already signed or for talent he or she would like to sign and then sell the project to an appropriate publisher. The agent might begin the process of stimulating an indication of interest or a verbal commitment from a publisher and then approach the talent, whether signed or not, or vice versa. Of course, the agent would not approach talent already signed with other agents or agencies.

Opportunities of many different kinds exist for precipitating large fees. However, there are certain pitfalls that must be avoided. For example, in many states, only licensed brokers and salespeople may be paid in connection with the purchase or sale of real property and this exclusion applies in some jurisdictions to all transactions involving real property, including the arranging of financing. In order for you, as an unlicensed real estate person, to be paid, you would be well advised to have an attorney (who is ordinarily permitted to collect fees in connection with real estate transactions) draw an agreement with the side of the transaction from whom payment is expected and include you in the payment to him or her on an agreed and lawful basis. Although it is my experience that most of the transactions in which money is precipitated do not require licenses it is a good idea to consult with a competent attorney so that a strong, valid agreement may be drawn which defines your payment.

Opportunities for precipitating money usually arise in one or a combination of relatively few circumstances. There may be a temporary imbalance of orders on the supply or demand side of the market in a particular commodity or finished goods generally or in a specific marketplace. You may be in a position to circumvent the normal channels of distribution, which are temporarily strained to overload by finding the side of the transaction in short supply. You may, either directly or indirectly, have the particular government connections through which a large purchase or sale may be channeled. Sometimes, government officials arrange sizable transactions through third parties as a means of having certain people participate in fees and/or commissions which they might not otherwise share. You should be sure you do not involve yourself in any improper or illegal activities in this regard.

You may, as I have, come into contact with a successful entrepreneur who wants to go into a business in a new field and who may profit by your expertise in that area. In my case, I heard of a man who wanted to buy and distribute made-for-television movies. As I knew a great deal about that business and had access to the independent producers from whom the properties would be purchased, I called the entrepreneur's colleague and set up a meeting. Within a relatively short time, a colleague and I were able to facilitate the purchases of several properties. As my colleague and I were flexible and knowledgeable and one of us was prepared to book a flight almost anywhere within reason the same day, if necessary, and as the entrepreneur was willing and able to make a financial commitment quickly and didn't need the approval of a board of directors or anybody else to do so, and as the offers were sensible, we were repeatedly able to outmaneuver our less nimble competitors, including several companies listed on the New York Stock Exchange. The deals were attractive and profitable to all of the parties, the entrepreneur, the production companies with which we dealt, and to my colleague and me.

You may have, or be able to develop, contacts within a foreign government and thereby receive a concession or preferred status not generally available, which gives you needed leverage with which to close deals. This may sound more unusual than it is. A friend has put together a number of successful transactions via this route, and I am currently examining a situation that appears to have enormous potential, which involves a concession from a foreign government. Opportunities for precipitating money may be found in securing underwriters for the purpose of taking companies public. I have acted as such a finder and received thousands of shares of stock in the underwritten company as my fee. You may encounter business people who are ill or elderly and who do not wish, or are unable, to travel long distances and deal in foreign countries but who have large sums of money and/or strong contacts and would like to engage in international commerce of one kind or another. Such situations have been offered to me and, although I have so far chosen not to enter this aspect of the game, it remains a possibility.

There are scores of additional opportunities for precipitating large fees. You may simply be able to match specific needs of which you are or become aware through direct association with a principal on one side of the transaction, or a middle person may present a similar opportunity. Large purchase orders, for example, can be accommodated if proper banking arrangements for assuring payment are in place, especially if the transaction will not upset existing patterns of distribution. If you represent the buy side, cash is king. If you are on the sell side, you would be in a position to deliver standardized goods in temporary short supply or at an attractive discount, or both.

In fact, in some cases, you may begin with neither side of the transaction and successfully seek both sides, as I have. Your approach should be to perform as great a function as you can to facilitate the closing of a deal, not simply to introduce two people. As many people are often less than excellent communicators, one of your functions may be to keep the channels of communication open and to facilitate the progress of the deal by promoting mutual understanding. I have been able to guide deals past sticking points in this way.

There are people in the real world who are relatively sensible within their accustomed environments but who, perhaps motivated by greed or ego needs, continually fatten imaginary parts for themselves in nonexistent money-precipitation dramas. These productions, composed solely of gossamer and verbiage, and utterly without a shred of redeeming substance, may be seriously offered to you. It is important that you not be caught up in them. The offerors enjoy talking about big deals and fantasying huge fees for themselves, an understandable failing, but one which might better be confined indoors away from means of communication.

Somehow, in the course of seeking to close phantom deals or deals in which these people are at or near the end of a long chain of increasingly less involved players, they may be led to call upon you and to invite your participation. Although the deal is at best vague, their manner may be surprisingly exact and even exacting. You may be asked, if the buy side is being sought, to establish the bona fides of the buyer in sometimes needlessly expensive, almost always time-consuming, and always embarrassing, ways, if for no other reason that that the other side of the transaction either doesn't exist at all or the deal is almost unrecognizably different from the way it has been presented to you. Although the size of the transaction is usually colossal (having been inflated en passant by other elements in the long chain of middle people), and the rationale for the alleged existence of the transaction bizarre, the details are stated with great precision, often in the lingo or patois of the deal-making cognoscenti.

A rule I have found most serviceable in these cases is to explain that before I am willing to get price quotations or provide banking instructions or expose my hand or, in fact, do anything that involves even a local telephone call, I must be satisfied as to the existence of an actual opportunity and of my position in it. This may require dealing directly with the principal on the side of the deal being presented (a chore I leave to the presenter to arrange), the exchanging of binding written agreements, the production of verified warehouse receipts, perhaps even the physical inspection of the goods if this is feasible. If the presenter purports to be speaking for an alleged buyer, at a minimum I would expect to be supplied with bona fide evidence the alleged buyer were ready, willing and able to make the purchase and a tight contract setting forth my fee and assuring it.

If I am not dealing directly with a principal, I put the burden on the other side to establish the existence of a genuine deal in the form presented. In this way, the evidence comes to me. I don't assume the task of seeking out the evidence as this is needlessly costly and time-consuming. Sometimes, in doubtful cases, if all else fails, and the middle person presenting the deal insists he or she is in earnest, I impose a simple demand that has never failed to terminate all further discussions. Deals presented by fantasists are almost invariably gigantic in size as it is as easy to discuss billion-dollar deals that don't exist as it is smaller deals. I have never concluded a multi-billion-dollar deal, although a number of non-existent opportunities of this magnitude have been offered to me. In addition, I've had some untoward experiences with billion-dollar presentations that have been notably absent from deals involving only millions.

In one case in which billions were seriously discussed with me, a presenter vouched for by a famous lawyer offered a deal in which I had sufficient lack of faith to pass. I was subsequently not surprised to read that the offeror had defrauded offerees of such deals of large sums of money. Other billion-dollar discussions have been equally unproductive. The simple demand I impose which discourages such inquiries (about price quotations, letters of credit and other commerical instruments and numerous similar requests that seek to elicit information or to establish the bona fides of my side of the transaction before the deal itself and my position in it has been firmly established as real) is to require that, prior to my becoming involved in a situation that seems incredible on its face, ten thousand dollars (or some other appropriate sum) be deposited by a principal on the other side of the transaction with an attorney as a forefeit if my efforts provide what is being sought and the other side fails to go forward.

The precipitation of money, as has been suggested, is largely dependent upon personal relationships. All of the other necessary elements are rather easily acquired. You may be required to pay relatively modest fees for professional assistance or you may trade away a percentage of your interest in the deal but help is available to you. The key element is people.

If you become a successful money precipitator you will discover that some people have an ability or knack for closing such deals and do so repeatedly; others are never able to precipitate a single fee try as they may. Your file of people with whom money precipitation is possible will be continually changing through additions and deletions. With experience, you will become more discerning. As in all other business relationships, you will want to avoid low-density people. They not only tend to waste time, money and energy, they also affect your credibility and this game requires that you maintain an extremely high degree of credibility. There is a great tendency to deal on the telephone, an admittedly inexpensive and efficient procedure. If, however, a deal begins to heat up, you should arrange to meet the players face to face. Disembodied voices may be deceptive. You will be much better able to assess the cast of characters in person.

Assemble a network of high-density people on whom you may call for the purpose of precipitating money. You must come to high-density people well prepared with a business proposal that you have thoroughly checked. Do not attempt to present incompletely thought out ideas to high-density people and expect the latter to do all of the preliminary work. They won't do it and you will lose face and undercut your relationship with them. You must be selective and thoroughly prepared. Do the homework yourself, or at least check it personally if you delegate the actual work to others.

You already know people who can precipitate money and/or you know people who know such money precipitators. You will undoubtedly meet others who can precipitate money and who can facilitate this process for you. You should begin to build a file of such people and develop a sensitivity to such people for future reference. If you do not already have business or calling cards, have some made up. If you prefer, you may have only your name and a telephone number on your cards. In any case, spend a few extra dollars and have some cards of excellent quality made for you. Avoid gimmicky cards and stay with white stock.

If you are not readily available during the day, and the precipitation of money often crosses time zones and lengthens the business day, you may want to buy a telephone answering machine or hire an answering service, with or without a paging service. If you decide on an answering service, be selective and make your need for courteous and competent service known at the outset, as such services vary greatly in performance levels. A good service will try to answer your telephone on the precise ring you specify (third, fourth, etcetera) and greet the caller exactly as you wrote the line. Monitor the service to determine whether your specifications are being met.

When you meet people who impress you and with whom you think you would enjoy doing business in the future, let them know you would like to see them again. Offer your card at a propitious moment. Be selective. Don't press. Don't hand out five cards at a time. This lowers the value of the card and others may tend to back away. Be aware of the connections between and among people who interest you. This is where your file folders and Rolodex (mentioned in a previous chapter) will play a part.

If you meet prospective associates at a mutual friend's home, it will be easy to contact them again, if you cannot do so directly. In asking your host or hostess for help you are not being indiscreet and your intentions are honorable. Your purpose is to create a project in which you and they (and perhaps your host or hostess) will benefit. Be aware of the proprieties and conventions. Some social functions are virtual extensions of business settings and such discussions are unexceptionable. Other social occasions may not be seized upon for business purposes of any kind without establishing those so engaged as pariahs. Discretion is always the best policy and an office visit or business lunch is a much more suitable setting for discussing business than a dinner party. If in doubt, don't push the conversation toward a deal in a social setting. There is no need to do so and it may be counterproductive to attempt it.

If you have a contribution to make to the kind of deal that might involve you in an open-ended competition with others, such as the financing of a transaction, for example, your efforts may prove successful but somebody else may be the one to close the deal and be paid. In such cases, particularly if you are not being paid anything for your time or out-of-pocket expenses, try to get an exclusive right to do whatever it is that is expected of you, at least for a reasonable, stated period of time, and a non-exclusive right thereafter. Get this in writing, properly authorized. It is frustrating to have the deal in hand only to be told the principal has made his or her arrangement away from you.

As the most ironclad contracts are sometimes contested, it should be clear that verbal agreements are even more likely not to be honored. It is also difficult to ask a third party or a judge to interpret a verbal agreement when the parties disagree about what was said. You will therefore want to secure a written agreement in almost all cases so that your participation, if not assured, is at least much more likely, should your efforts be successful.

Keep accurate records on how much time and money you spend in quest of money precipitation. If the rewards are not forthcoming or are not commensurate with the outlays and the expenses become onerous, you are under no obligation to continue to play this particular game. Learn from your mistakes. Keep weeding out the people who lack or lose credibility or are overly time-consuming. Insist that proposals come to you well prepared. Be selective. Don't automatically assume all of the expenses for your efforts. If travel expenses are to be incurred, for example, discuss with the presenter how this item should be handled. High-density deal-makers don't expect you to incur thousands of dollars of expenses on speculations they present. Others, whatever their good qualities, are not likely to precipitate money with you, so you have little to lose by clarifying how the larger expense items are to be handled.

The precipitation of money is a heady game. I have participated in it with pleasure and profit and I know others who have precipitated six- and seven-figure sums for themselves in deals not directly connected with their business or profession. These are the kinds of rewards that may well be within your own reach.

XVI

...To You and Your Heirs Forever

The subject of how to maximize your net, after-tax, income, how to accumulate and augment your net worth, and how to transfer your wealth in accordance with your wishes and the needs of those affected, during your lifetime and in the event of your death, legally keeping as much of your wealth as possible beyond the reach of tax collectors is, or should be, of interest to most income producers and their heirs and other beneficiaries. Before continuing, a broad disclaimer is in order. Tax planning and estate planning are complex subjects. Each is governed by changing laws and interpretations of laws. In addition, specific plans tailored to individual needs and objectives provide optimum results. This is the essence of sound planning. An unmarried, unemployed nineteen-year-old student's needs and objectives will almost undoubtedly differ greatly from those of a ninety-one-year-old mogul. This chapter could not be, and is not intended to be, prescriptive advice to be followed by every reader regardless of his or her circumstances and objectives, nor is it designed for any particular reader. It is, rather, meant to indicate the importance of tax and estate planning, to point up the significant differences such planning may contribute to your own financial security and that of those close to you, and to look at some of the benefits currently available. This sort of planning deserves the attention of every reader of a book on the subject of acquiring wealth. If this material stimulates such interest it will have achieved its primary goal.

This treatment of tax and estate planning has three natural divisions: 1) How to decrease taxes on earned income and use the tax savings to produce additional wealth that is, in turn, also tax-sheltered. This aspect of tax planning attempts to provide greater wealth for its participants while avoiding high-risk investments. 2) How to use so-called tax-shelter investments to reduce taxes on current and future earnings. This involves a higher degree of risk in many cases and is ordinarily of interest to those in relatively high tax brackets. 3) How to transfer wealth in accordance with the wishes of the transferor and the needs of the transferee, at the same time legally avoiding the payment of as much gift and estate taxes as is practicable.

A great deal of publicity is given periodically to the fact that a particular wealthy person, or a list of them, paid little or no federal income taxes in a given year or over a stated period of time, despite an income several times that of yours or mine. Congress has enacted several laws designed to encourage certain types of investments deemed beneficial to a broad cross section of the public. A major incentive for the implementation of such policies is the creation of tax benefits. Among the benefits are some that are not only for the very rich but are of potential value to virtually every taxpayer, whether an employee of a large or small company, a government employee, a professional, a self-employed person, an employee of a tax-exempt institution, a part-time or temporary worker, a farmer, or whether gainfully employed in almost any other job category. Even unemployed people who intend to become employed may benefit from this aspect of tax planning. Precisely how you should formulate your own tax plans so that your net earned income is maximized and its growth is promoted is an individual matter which will best be decided after consulting a competent tax planner but it may be helpful to consider some of the broad strokes.

Although only about ten percent of the so-called labor force are considered to be self-employed, I prefer to begin with the benefits available to such people as they are presumably in a position to have a plan designed for themselves that takes advantage of a great number of these benefits. By forming a corporation (which you may do even if you are its only employee) and becoming an employee of that corporation you are entitled to participate in a number of benefits the corporation may create for you. For example, the corporation may establish a qualified pension and/or profit-sharing plan through which, if both are set up, a total of up to 25 percent of the annual salary the corporation pays you (including bonus and commissions), may be contributed. The corporation would pay no taxes on the amounts thus paid into one or both of these plans and neither would you, the employee, until the funds were paid out to you, beginning at age fifty-nine and a half or at any time thereafter up to age seventy.

You may elect to take a lump sum payout and deposit the entire sum in an individual retirement account (IRA) and pay no taxes on the "rollover" until you begin to collect from the IRA. The funds in your profit and/or profit-sharing plan(s) might be invested in a wide variety of ways and you might choose to appoint yourself trustee of one or both plans and make all of the investment decisions if you so desired. As all of the increments (capital gains, dividends, interest, etcetera) would likewise be tax-free until the funds were paid out (and the payout might be arranged in a variety of ways, at your election), it would be in your interest to invest these sums rather conservatively and make less conservative investments, if desired, with taxable dollars so that the taxing authorities shared the risks with you, as it were.

As an example of how the pension and profit-sharing plans might work, suppose you created eighty thousand dollars of gross pre-tax income in a given year. The federal income tax you would have to pay, plus possible state and local income tax as well, on the last sixteen thousand dollars of your taxable income would be lost to you and your heirs forever, as would all of the money you could earn with this sum if it could be saved. As an employee of a corporation that had pension and profit-sharing plans in which you participated, your corporation might pay you a salary of sixty-four thousand dollars (on which you would pay considerably less tax) and put a total of sixteen thousand dollars into your plans without paying any corporate tax whatever and deferring all taxes on the amounts paid in as well as the increments on these amounts until much later in the game when you would likely be in a lower tax bracket or might arrange otherwise to shelter this income.

Your corporation might offer a stock purchase plan that permitted you to buy stock with a certain percentage of your gross salary plus sales commissions and sales bonuses and the corporation might add a certain percentage of your contribution as a contribution of its own. Both you and the corporation would contribute pre-tax dollars and you would be purchasing the stock at a discount by virtue of the corporate contribution. All of the increments, including dividends, would accumulate tax-free until either you retired or until the occurrence of some other specified event such as death, disability or resignation from the company. The corporation normally pays for the administration of the plan, does all of the bookkeeping, reduces stock commissions by buying in large quantities and pays the trustee for administering the plan. You also enjoy the benefit of dollar cost averaging. This technique involves the purchase of a security at regular intervals with the same amount of money. By buying more shares at lower prices and fewer shares at higher prices with the same fixed amount, this method will produce a lower average price per share than would the purchase of the same number of shares at the same intervals. The same sort of plan might be drawn up by your corporation with the exception that cash would be contributed and accumulated for you instead of stock.

In addition, your corporation might provide for a voluntary contribution plan into which you would be permitted to contribute up to ten percent of your gross annual corporate salary (including sales bonuses and sales commissions) into a trust over which you might, if you chose, be named trustee so that you would be able to make the investment decisions. These contributions would be in after-tax dollars but all of the increments would accumulate untaxed in the same manner as the assets in your pension and/or profit-sharing plan.

Your corporation might also pay you cash and/or stock bonuses, grant you stock options, defer some of your compensation to later years when, presumably, you would be in a lower income tax bracket, and buy life, medical, dental, accident and disability insurance for you, among other so-called fringe benefits and perks. Similar benefits are available to certain professionals (doctors, lawyers and others) depending upon state law governing which professionals may and may not incorporate. The letters "P.C.," for Professional Corporation, after the names of these professionals on their letterheads, cards and the nameplates outside their offices, indicate this election, which is being made increasingly.

Not nearly as valuable but certainly better than no retirement plan at all is the Individual Retirement Account (IRA). If your employer has not established a qualified retirement plan that includes you or you have not become a participant in such a plan, you may set up an IRA and contribute up to 15 percent of your annual salary, up to a maximum of $1,500. If your spouse is not employed, the maximum is increased to $1,750 per year. Your contribution is in pre-tax dollars and all of the increments accumulate untaxed until they are paid out. There are various options as to types of investments that may be made, methods of payout, and a provision for transferring a lump sum payout of a qualified pension and/or profit-sharing plan on a tax-deferred basis within a specified period of time (and vice versa), as well as the transfer of funds from one type of IRA to another. Local banks may supply specific details on the Individual Retirement Accounts they offer.

Self-employed individuals may participate in so-called Keogh retirement plans without incorporating. Such persons may contribute up to 15 percent of their earned income annually (up to a maximum of $7,500) without paying a tax on the contribution. These contributions to the plan and all increments accumulate free of tax until they are paid out. There are choices to be made as to what kinds of investments may be made with the funds and who shall act as administrator of the funds.

You may fine-tune a benefit package for yourself if you control your own corporation or professional corporation. If you are unemployed and intend to seek employment, you may find a number of significant differences in the benefit plans available to you among otherwise rather similar employment opportunities that, in the aggregate, will produce an enormous disparity in your net worth over the course of several years. Furthermore, there are many benefits and perks available to so-called key executives in a great number of large and medium-sized corporations that are unavailable to other employees. These opportunities present shortcuts for the accumulation of substantial wealth and should not be overlooked by valued and experienced personnel, whether negotiating a job change or a job title change or whenever an opportunity can be developed. These special benefits may be bargained for separately if you have or attain a certain status or job title or salary level. Regardless of your employment status, however, a familiarity with what is available not only in your company or industry but what legislators have deliberately and consciously put in place to help you increase your net worth, and how these benefits have been extended by others, may make an important difference in the amount of financial security you, and those closest to you, have in future years.

The total benefit package you may create for yourself, both through self-employment or through outside employment, deserves your attention. In a growing number of companies, precisely the kind of estate and tax planning advice you may find extremely valuable is available as an additional fringe benefit. If this benefit is not available, your attorney or accountant may be able to suggest a competent professional you may consult for a relatively modest fee. Some preparatory reading material may be obtained from the International Association of Financial Planners, 2150 Parklake Drive, N.E., Atlanta, Georgia 30345, tel. 404–934–0533.

In addition to the kinds of tax benefits already referred to, there are a number of so-called tax-shelter investments. In general terms, such investments involve either 1) a tax-free return (like the interest on municipal bonds); or, 2) they are designed to produce tax deductions from current income, whether earned or unearned, deductions from future investment income, and/or the opportunity to sell the investment at a profit that will generate capital gains. The purpose of the second kind of tax-shelter investment is to yield a return fully or partly free of tax and to provide enough deductions and/or credits to reduce current taxes.

The mechanism of these tax-shelter investments lies in a provision of the tax laws that permits expenses made in the course of profit-oriented activities to be treated as deductions and/or credits. A method of maximizing these deductions and credits is the so-called leverage derived from borrowed funds. The shelter is usually intended to produce a net loss, during the early years of the investment, that may be used to offset other income and thus reduce taxes which otherwise would be owing. In later years, if the project is successful, net income will be produced, some or all of which may also be tax-free for a number of years by virtue of depletion, depreciation and/ or other legal means of offsetting income in the particular shelter.

This is not to imply that all tax-shelter investments are profitable. A favorable outcome of such investments would be to reduce taxes you would otherwise have to pay on income and short-term capital gains, after which the investment would produce income for you tax-free for several years. However, there are a number of risks inherent in many tax-shelter vehicles which must be taken into account.

The Internal Revenue Service might attack the entire investment or challenge certain aspects of it. The promoters, salespersons and/or managers may be overpaid, dishonest and/or incompetent. The project may be unsound or conditions might sufficiently change so that the investment proved to be unprofitable. The project might be so unsuccessful it would have to be liquidated.

In short, the risks inherent in tax-shelter investments span a broad spectrum from relatively low to prohibitively high. It is possible, in a given instance, to invest in a share of the worst of both worlds; i.e., you lose both the desired tax benefits as well as your investment. The higher your tax bracket, the less painful the losses, as the taxing authorities are, in effect, sharing them with you to some extent. At the same time, the potential benefits are greater for those in higher tax brackets.

In any case, a rather conservative approach is recommended by most experts in the field with whom I've spoken. The character, experience and competence of the creators, sellers and managers of the investment must be scrutinized before you invest. The legal and economic soundness of the investment and its appropriateness for you must be appraised. Legal and tax advisers in whom you have confidence and who are not connected with the investment should be consulted. Tax-shelter investments may be ideal for some people but there are a number of pitfalls for the unwary. For most people, the less exotic investments may be preferable, such as, for example, the ownership of one's own home and various other real estate investments.

In addition to managing your financial affairs so that you legally net as much of your income as you prudently can, sound financial planning includes consideration of how to conserve, augment and transfer income and other items of wealth, to the extent feasible and desirable, so that taxes are reduced and your intentions and the interests of those you wish to benefit are well served. Trusts and estates, wills, gifts, leasebacks after gift or sale, and the various taxes involved in such transfers, are the basic elements to be considered in formulating a comprehensive estate plan. The realization of long-term objectives are involved in estate planning. The planners are attempting to look at least into the next generation. These objectives will change as you and those for whom you are planning grow older, as circumstances change, and as your needs, and the needs of those for whom you are attempting to provide, change. In addition, there are likely to be new laws enacted, changes in the law and shifts of interpretation of applicable laws over the long term which may require changes in your estate plan. There are so many variations and variables and the consequences of this or that action may be so far-reaching that I strongly recommend not only that much thought be given to formulating your plans and to their effective review and updating, but also to your choice of advisers. In the following material, I have arbitrarily selected some of the highlights that may be of general interest.

Prior to January, 1977, you were permitted to give $3,000 per year to as many people as you chose and you also had a lifetime exemption of $30,000 which you might give, all without the imposition of any gift tax. If you were married and your spouse agreed (even if none of the funds belonged to your spouse), the annual tax-free gift and the lifetime exemption were each doubled to $6,000 per person and $60,000. The law has been changed. The $3,000 ($6,000 with spouse approval) gifts may still be made (in after-tax dollars) free of gift tax (and the donee pays no income tax) but the lifetime exemption has been eliminated and replaced with a credit of $47,000 against gift taxes that may be due.

Sharing income-producing property with family members may greatly increase the total net, after tax, dollars of the family. Gifts of property that have appreciated in value (or which you think will appreciate) may save capital gains tax. Another effective device is the sale and leaseback or the gift and leaseback, by which the high tax bracket owner sells or gives property to a low-income tax bracket family member who leases it back to the former owner. Rents accrue to the low-income tax bracket new owner and are deductible as expenses to the former owner, lowering his or her tax burden. Tax savings may also be effected through the establishment of one or more trusts that accumulate income from property placed in trust by a high tax bracket individual for the benefit of a low-income tax bracket person.

In the past, such high-tax-bracket individuals often used the Clifford Trust for reducing taxes on income-producing property (stocks that paid dividends, bonds that paid interest, real estate that paid rents, etcetera), often for the purpose of paying for a child's college education with dollars that would otherwise be taxed away. After a period of time (which had to be at least ten years unless the grantee died sooner) the property would revert to the grantor. However, during the term of the trust, the income would accumulate for the child and be taxed at the child's (or other beneficiary of the trust) zero or low tax rate. Short-term trusts, including the Clifford Trust, are not as attractive for some taxpayers because the Tax Reform Act of 1976 made the transfer of a ten-year (or longer) interest on the income a taxable gift. However, the Clifford Trust as it now stands still offers advantages for many, if not all, taxpayers and it may be combined with other devices to produce most of the objectives it formerly achieved.

Virtually every estate planner worthy of the name will be able to give you several reasons for having a will regardless of how large or small your estate may be. I prefer not to list the standard reasons in favor of recommending you ask any professional in this field whose opinion you value.

Many people are good at producing large incomes and a great deal of wealth but below average at accumulating such wealth and poor at transferring it. Production, accumulation and transfer of wealth require somewhat different combinations of skills. There are several documented cases of estates of wealthy people that were needlessly taxed millions of dollars because of some elementary error or omission. Good planning and continuing supervision with competent and reliable professionals should promote your objectives and eliminate unnecessary penalties of this kind.

The purpose of this chapter is not to attempt to list a number of courses of action that might well be obsoleted before you can benefit from them or to set forth questionable gimmicks that are on or over the edge of the law, but to suggest that tax and estate planning are vital to your accumulation of wealth and to the future financial security of those you love. It is better to begin too early than too late to design your own plans and you will need good advice. The magic of thinking rich would be only a shell game unless the fruits of your success are enjoyed by you and your heirs for many, many years to come.

XVII

Not by Bread Alone

In these pages it has been my intention to present the best approach I know to making you wealthy: the magic of thinking rich as an amalgam of attitudinal and practical approaches to the acquisition of riches. It is not a closed system, like Euclidian geometry, for example, but an open system, like life itself. As in a well-adapted organism, the parts are interrelated and work well in concert, in combination. The wealth you are able to create, however, is only a part of your life. It is a valuable tool that can be used creatively to enhance the enjoyment of your life, not, it is hoped, sought for its own sake and used to cut you off from life itself.

There is a spirit in the magic of thinking rich that consists in a creative relationship with others and with all of the elements in your environment context. The wealth and prosperity thus created are by-products of these relationships. In a creative relationship, you become rich not by taking more from others than is your due or giving them less than their fair share but by doing precisely the reverse. In a creative environment, others do not execute your ideas and projects because of fear or force but because they have an interest in making a contribution. You and they are free to express yourselves and to achieve together. A money magician is an artist not a trickster. His or her work, like his or her life, is approached creatively. There is no trickery, no deceit, no cheating or stealing in money magic.

Character and mental attitude will determine most of the outcomes of the situations you will face in your life. In a series of daily choices you make, your character is created. Your character is the cutting edge of the most important possession you have: yourself. It is the vital tool with which you approach the world. If it is defective or brittle or unbalanced or encrusted with barnacles, it is incapable of producing optimum results for you. Such a character will lower your consciousness, and your total environment, the world you create for yourself, will mirror this impaired character and lowered consciousness. Your portion will be accordingly smaller. Your life will become constricted and dimmed and you will lose wholeheartedness and zest. If this condition is allowed to continue, you will be driven by anxiety. Loss and pain will probably follow and your character may be expected to deteriorate further. These will be reflected in your attitudes and actions and the process will feed on itself as your life winds down to a joyless existence.

You can halt this self-defeating process.

Observe what works well for yourself and others. The late Joseph Wood Krutch declared that, "We have been deluded by the fact that the methods employed for the study of man have been, for the most part, those originally devised for the study of machines or the study of rats, and are capable, therefore, of detecting and measuring only those characteristics which the three do have in common." Study the best models and learn from them. If somebody is extraordinary or exhibits some remarkable characteristic you find compelling, discover what gives you that impression. What is that person doing or not doing that communicates this to you? What sensory data have thus affected you? By observing differences and making choices you may steer yourself in any desired direction.

The magic of thinking rich involves an active approach to life, a loyalty to your best self, a fidelity to your ideals, and a living movement toward your potentials. It does not involve waiting for a miracle or wasting or squandering your resources but using them creatively. It involves will and action and enterprise and excellence. It is a movement toward independence. It is a reliance more and more on the self and less and less on props and settings. A country doctor makes house calls with only a small black medical bag and his or her self yet the skilled practitioner is equipped to diagnose and treat an extraordinary variety of medical problems. If the patient does not respond to one modality of treatment, the doctor will use another in an effort to promote a favorable response. The more strategies in his or her repertoire, the more observant and skilled the doctor, the higher the success rate is likely to be.

Too many people rely on too few strategies in approaching the various situations in their lives. Sometimes their strategies are effective; often they are not. Additional strategies are needed but the individual has simply not learned the behaviors that will provide the desired results. The result is a diminished personal reality.

In these pages I have set forth all of the basic behaviors and strategies successful people use over and over again to produce wealth. If you widen your choices by adding these behaviors to your own repertoire and are willing to work at it diligently, you can produce a reality of wealth for yourself hitherto only a stubborn hope or wish or dream. This work is intended not as a secret formula or a blueprint but as a map of the terrain. How you arrive at your own destination of wealth is up to you. I have emphasized principles and positions so that a practical course may be more easily adapted by skillful players to meet changing circumstances and conditions.

If you are willing to accept complete responsibility for your current financial position as a given, without rancor or rationalization, you thereby free your energies to set about the removal of all of the self-made obstacles to your productivity and prosperity. Only by cutting yourself free of past failures and disappointments and bad conditioning are you able to adapt and respond to the actual playing conditions on the field while the game is still in progress. Nobody can take his or her best swing at the ball while replaying in their imagination their last strikeout.

The reason most people cannot go the distance to great wealth is not that they are incapable of so doing but that they are unwilling, for whatever reasons, to do the preparation. Those who adequately prepare, usually finish the race and some set world records. Finishing the race, in the context of the magic of thinking rich, means becoming wealthy; adequate preparation means developing the character and the personal style and the knowledge to make it happen for you.

The acquisition of big money is a serious matter. It requires time and energy and discipline as well as attitude and style and knowledge. It does not, however, require an exclusive, unbalanced, slavish commitment. In fact, the tunnel vision of such a monomaniacal approach would be counterproductive of great wealth. Overzealousness does not attract great success. Limiting your field of vision narrows the basis on which you are able to make decisions and is restrictive and limiting. On the other hand, when a particular behavior seems to work, there is a temptation to repeat it as the expense of self-development, the discovering of other adaptive behaviors. There is a tendency to rationalize the postponement of the development of other aspects of a rounded life until later, after you're rich.

Avoid this trap. Your life is not a series of discrete points like the glows of a thousand fireflies. It is a continuum, and if you fail to integrate into this continuum the important and nurturing elements of love, friendship and the human spirit and a spirituality which places you in a larger context, and a love of nature and the arts, your humanity atrophies. The continuum doesn't stop but you shrink and become diminished as a person. If you ever do become rich, you may find your capacity for enjoying the high levels of happiness that should be available to you are seriously impaired.

You have the power to choose your life-style, not tomorrow, not five years from now when you get rich, but right now. This is the most important choice you have and yet many are unaware of its reality and its urgency. By making decisions about what you value and exercising choices about how you spend your time and thought and energy, by deciding what you will or will not incorporate and integrate into your life, and how you will shape and order these elements, you create your life-style.

Life is greater than, and will outgrow, any compartment in which it is placed. Life involves flux, it is in continual change, and if you fail to grow and develop, you will be choosing not to be fully functioning, fully alive in life. There is a voice within each of us that cries out for the way it might be. In those who have not learned to listen to this lone, inner voice, it becomes muted or sullen, perhaps even stilled. This voice must be nurtured and strengthened so that its urgent messages are heard and heeded. It is in this voice that your individuality, your person, your very being, is centered. Find and follow this wise child within and you can be whole and happy, free at last to be the best you can be and to live in harmony with yourself and your universe. Ignore this call, or fail to heed it, and you impair yourself as a person.

It is better to become rich surely than swiftly, through energy and principle than rapacity or dishonesty. The magic in the magic of thinking rich doesn't refer to a magic wand. It implies method, direction, drive, perseverence. It means breaking all of the binding chains of hopelessness and rage and pain.

Big money, as was stated in the first chapter of this work, is many things to many people. It is a tool and a tranquilizer, it is warmth and safety, it is privacy and comfort, it is ease and luxury. It is freedom from want and fear. It is never having to say you're sorry to yourself or to those you love. It is entree and serenity. It is the best of the world's goods and services and a life of great opportunities and pleasures for you and your heirs forever. Big money is, indeed, all of these and more but money alone is not enough to produce completeness, wholeness, a unified, integrated, balanced life of harmony, development and happiness. Opportunities, pleasures, yes; but a full life requires more.

Harmony and happiness imply a life in which the individual is not continually engaged in a state of conflict with his or herself or with elements of his or her environment. The ordinary person is conscious of his or herself as being in a position apart, separated from the world in which he or she lives. He or she is involved in an unceasing effort to control or manipulate the myriad elements with which he or she comes in contact. Unforeseen elements intrude to upset this delicate balance. The process continues, and finally he or she either retires from the struggle in despair or continues this unsuccessful battle with a self-created hostile environment.

You may go beyond this self-imposed chaos by becoming unified with your own nature and with all that had previously been viewed as outside of yourself. Unless this is accomplished, no amount of money alone or of any other buttressing from outside of yourself will be more than temporarily availing. Such a fragmented person either gives up on his or herself or continually seeks outside confirmation and support, repeatedly self-imposing more and more difficult tasks until an impasse is finally created. The end result of this internal disharmony is a loss of creativity, a lack of zest, a kind of living death in which the individual's own being is blocked or destroyed.

The living solution lies in an authenticity of person, of being, of action, that relies on no false props, on nothing beyond the reality, the living fact, that one is part of a larger context that cannot be betrayed without betraying part of oneself. It is important to remember in this connection, as you become wealthy, that money is fungible; any given sum is much like any other equal sum. However, all that is living is unique and must be preserved.

Once you discover your own identity and make the connection between that identity and a source beyond the self, your life takes on an authenticity, an enrichment, a new reality. This rich, burnished life becomes unbounded, part of a continuum, part of a process that is never finished. You reach this understanding, as with other valuable realizations, not be intellectualizing, but only after a personal engagement with life, a struggle from which you emerge as part of, and unified with, that with which you were struggling, unified with life itself.

After this struggle has been undergone, you become free to take your place in the world. The elements you thereafter encounter in the world are not manipulated or avoided, but experienced and related to in a new appreciation of their unique being and with due regard to their nature. Thus enlightened by your personal engagement and struggle, you incorporate the realization that the more of yourself that goes into a relationship, the more creative, the more alive, it is. Holding yourself apart from a relationship, attempting to preserve yourself from change, from risk, from life itself, in effect, destroys a creative relationship.

As you enter into a creative relationship with life, you also avoid uncreative relationships. All that is false or not true to yourself is thus avoided. This includes all that is secondhand, that has not been made your own by direct relationship, by actual use, by living with it. All that is not truly your own in this sense is stripped off and discarded.

By thus returning to what is your own irreducible self, you are left with what is undeniably yours, that which nobody can take away; namely, your own identity, your very self and being. As you interact with life from the bedrock of what is completely and uniquely your own, you are able to enter situations according to your nature. You are thus freed of all of the false elements, the secondhand, the wholesale merchandise, the hand-me-downs you and others had been so ready to fasten onto you. You are freed to face life, to participate in your own being, creatively and wholeheartedly.

If you are the one reader in ten to whom I referred in the first chapter of this book, the reader for whom this book was written, and you have come this far, there is one more point I would make. We live in a materialistic culture and money is a valuable commodity, to be sure. However, your becoming a millionaire, even if you do it in the purest, most joyful and most guilt-free way, will not, in and of itself, solve all of your problems or make you truly happy permanently or for a relatively long time. Many years ago, a young woman told me that having sexual intercourse was a nice way of getting to know somebody. In the same way that having sexual intercourse may be a nice way of getting to know somebody, becoming wealthy may provide an opportunity for getting to know yourself and how you relate to a larger context; that is, all that which is not yourself. You have, no doubt, been touched by children who were open and honest and loving and lovable. If children can be so, why not adults? Why not you?

As an archery target becomes a focus for organizing activity for the purpose of projecting arrows at it, the goal of accumulating wealth stimulates and promotes other kinds of activities. The process of actually accumulating wealth is a kind of complex game. The better players of the wealth accumulation game receive serious sums of money as their respective prizes. The more enlightened among these players learn, in the process of acquiring money, that the world is bigger than their wealth accumulation game and, if they are so minded and have what it takes, they break out of the tunnel of their wealth accumulation game and discover that they are part of a universe of other games, other people, an entire natural world of vast interest and beauty, a variegated carnival of art and science and that the sights of their telescopes can be elevated to the very heavens.

About the Author

A former network television program executive and operator of a Wall Street securities firm that bore his name, Ralph Charell has been recognized by *The Guiness Book of World Records* as "the world's most successful complainer" and Knighted by The Mark Twain Society for his "outstanding contribution to American humor." He is the author of *How I Turn Ordinary Complaints into Thousands of Dollars, A Great New Way to Make Money, How to Get the Upper Hand* and *How to Make Things Go Your Way.*